ADVANCE PRAISE FOR

A Cross-Cultural Consideration of Teacher Leaders' Narratives of Power, Agency, and School Culture:

England, Jamaica, and the United States

"*A Cross-Cultural Consideration of Teacher Leaders' Narratives of Power, Agency, and School Culture* provides rich insights of the ways in which teachers lead in England, Jamaica and the United States. This book fills a void in the literature on teacher leadership, bringing the essential role of teachers as they use their power to enhance students' educational experience and shape school cultures for positive learning outcomes. Utilizing powerful stories about teachers' leadership across these three countries, Blair, Roofe, and Timmins show why teachers are the single most important aspect in students' educational attainment. This book is a must read for teachers, principals, parents, education officers, and those seeking to understand teachers' leadership across cultures."

Dr. K. Alexander Williams
Dean, School for International Training, The Graduate Institute

"Having had the privilege of working with many educational leaders in several countries, I have long realized that the issues are not dissimilar in nature and complexity. The text then is a helpful resource as it offers insights into the experiences of teacher leaders as shaped by their cultural realities."

Dr. Maurice D. Smith, JP
CPFEd, International Educational Consultant

"Blair, Roofe, and Timmins offer a powerful cross-cultural analysis of teacher leadership, school culture, and politics, and an exploration of the associated challenges faced within the US, England, and Jamaica—in part through teacher interviews within these three countries. The authors offer an assessment of the limitations—and the promise—of teacher leadership in these politically, historically, and educationally different contexts wherein consistently the teaching profession is underappreciated. This groundbreaking volume is essential because we need an understanding of—and full implementation of—teacher leadership in order to bring about meaningful shared leadership and significant school improvement. This is crucial reading also because the teaching/learning process at its essence is represented most significantly in the relationship between the teacher and the student—wherein the rubber meets the road."

Kofi Lomotey
Bardo Distinguished Professor
Western Carolina University

"If you want to understand teachers' work in the 21st century, and why we don't have the school workplaces that teachers desire, then this is the book for you. Veteran teacher-educators Blair, Roofe, and Timmins have crafted a stirring book for, about, and in defense of teachers that every parent, politician, and policy-maker must read as well as teachers and administrators. Their cross-cultural look at teachers' work in England, Jamaica, and the United States is brutally honest and incredibly hopeful about teachers as leaders in schools. With more than 60 combined years of experience teaching, supervising, and learning in school systems, they make a strong and compelling case for the transformation of schools as workplaces that position teachers as leaders who can use their power and agency for joyous, trusting, and equitable school cultures."

Hilton Kelly
Immediate Past President of the American Educational Studies Association
Chair of Educational Studies Department at Davidson College

A Cross-Cultural Consideration of Teacher Leaders' Narratives of Power, Agency, and School Culture

CRITICAL STUDIES IN TEACHER LEADERSHIP SERIES

Eleanor J. Blair, *Editor*

Teacher leadership as a term is used broadly to describe the many roles and responsibilities of good teachers working in 21st-century schools. Teacher leaders, acting in both formal and informal roles, are instrumental in doing at least three things: facilitating and sustaining teacher voice; building leadership capacity in schools and communities; and addressing teaching and learning issues and concerns with best practices, evidence, and research. Research on the intersection of teacher leadership, school culture, and school improvement is extremely limited, particularly as it pertains to school reform efforts that occur in diverse geographical and social contexts. Important factors that affect the work of teacher leaders include, but are not limited to, issues such as race; urban and rural education; socio-economics; ethnicity; politics; and ideological differences. Critical efforts to link teacher leadership with increased power and agency in teachers' work are limited. Teacher leadership that is both transformative and critical serves the purpose of redefining teachers' work to include new roles and responsibilities, such as advocacy leadership and a commitment to the principles of social justice as key components of teachers' work. As such, a better understanding of teacher leadership and the way that it functions in schools and communities has the potential to nurture new conceptualizations of the teaching profession, but also on the work of teachers advocating for both academic and social reform in public spaces for teaching and learning.

BOOKS IN THE SERIES

A Cross-Cultural Consideration of Teacher Leaders' Narratives of Power,
Agency, and School Culture: England, Jamaica, and the United States
by Eleanor J. Blair, Carmel Roofe, and Susan Timmons (2020)
Bridges, not Blockades: Transcending University Politics
by Gayle Wells-Maddox and Martha Diede (2020)
Stewarding the Profession: Stories of Early Career Teacher Leadership
by Carrie Rogers (2020)

Interested authors and collection editors are invited to contact:

Eleanor J. Blair
ejblair@email.wcu.edu

A Cross-Cultural Consideration of Teacher Leaders' Narratives of Power, Agency, and School Culture

England, Jamaica, and the United States

Edited by Eleanor J. Blair, Carmel Roofe,
and Susan Timmins

Myers
Education
Press

GORHAM, MAINE

Myers
Education
Press

Published by Myers Education Press, LLC
P.O. Box 424 Gorham, ME 04038

Myers Education Press is an academic publisher specializing in books, e-books, and digital content in the field of education. All of our books are subjected to a rigorous peer review process and produced in compliance with the standards of the Council on Library and Information Resources.

Library of Congress Cataloging-in-Publication Data available from Library of Congress.

13-digit ISBN 978-1-9755-0158-7 (paperback)
13-digit ISBN 978-1-9755-0157-0 (hard cover)
13-digit ISBN 978-1-9755-0159-4 (library networkable e-edition)
13-digit ISBN 978-1-9755-0160-0 (consumer e-edition)

Printed in the United States of America.

All first editions printed on acid-free paper that meets the American National Standards Institute Z39-48 standard.

Books published by Myers Education Press may be purchased at special quantity discount rates for groups, workshops, training organizations, and classroom usage. Please call our customer service department at 1-800-232-0223 for details.

Cover and text design by Sophie Appel.

Visit us on the web at **www.myersedpress.com** to browse our complete list of titles.

CONTENTS

Section Four: Cross-Cultural Considerations
of Teacher Leaders' Work

DEDICATIONS

To Charlotte Palmer Cannon: When I look in your eyes, I see hope for the future;
a future where teachers and the children they teach are valued and schools are
joyous places for everyone who enters their doors.
—EB

To the amazing Jamaican teachers who go above and beyond the call of duty
to inspire your students to achieve greatness, regardless of their circumstances
I salute you.
—CR

To all the teacher leaders in England, emerging or established,
keep striving to be the best you can be, for the good of the students that you teach
and the school communities in which you work.
—ST

FOREWORD

PAUL MILLER

IT IS WELL-KNOWN, ALTHOUGH perhaps not as well understood, that "The work of the teacher is many-sided and difficult" (Maxey, 1956, p. 264). It is also well-known that teachers are the single most important factor in the performance of students. Teachers work alongside other staff, in particular school leaders, to provide students with knowledge, skills, and other tools to support their effective functioning in society. Teachers, whether in developing and/or developed countries, have not always had the respect, support, and appreciation they deserve, and in many cases they have been blamed for almost everything that is wrong or has gone wrong with(in) an educational system. As noted in the *School Leadership for the 21st Century Initiative Report*, funded by the U.S.-based Institute for Educational Leadership (2001):

> Mischaracterized though they often are as incompetent know nothings, teachers are, paradoxically, education's "franchise players," its indispensable but unappreciated leaders in the truest meaning of the word. It is unarguable that they instill, mold, and ultimately control much of the learning and intellectual development of the young people in their charge. It would be difficult to find a more authentic but unacknowledged example of leadership in modern life. (p. 1)

There are several other examples, from research, of teachers feeling "demeaned," "degraded," "unfairly criticised," and "sick and tired of being asked to justify their existence" in the face of "constant government put downs" (p. 116). Nevertheless, they are foundational to the provision of education as well as to the stability and continuity of that provision in any country.

Globally, over the past two decades especially, the demands on schools and on teachers have become more complex and more exacting as national governments and policy-makers attempt to improve the performance and outcomes of national education systems. Schools and schooling are being swiftly reconfigured to be springboards for national economic development, simultaneously being responsive to a constantly changing student clientele and to the opportunities of new technologies. Schools therefore have an important role to play in national transformation agendas. As a result, teachers have to be available in good supply, and they must possess an appropriate mix of qualifications, skills, and experience. Importantly, as performativity agendas become much more firmly embedded in national education systems, and with mounting country-to-country and school-to-school competition, teachers are increasingly called upon to take on additional tasks in the management and leadership of schools. This important fact and feature of school leadership is arguably less readily apparent than other aspects of a teacher's duty related to the classroom. Accordingly, it has been noted that:

> Teachers do and can provide important scaffolding for school leaders and custodianship of teaching and learning. With more schools leveraging the experience and skills of teachers to increase their overall performance and therefore outcomes for students, the important role played by teachers both within and outside the classroom has taken on greater significance. (Miller, 2018, p. 81)

This important observation highlights the fact that a teacher's work is not entirely classroom based, and in undertaking their increasingly expanding portfolios, they perform important leadership roles—on a daily basis—in order to sustain their schools and its work. There are several overlapping roles associated with the work of teachers, among which "leadership" has been identified as central. This is important, since any one time, a teacher occupies multiple roles, simultaneously pointing to the fact that the work of schools and school leaders would be impossible without them, and further highlighting the fact that teachers perform leadership roles in multiple areas of a school in multiple ways.

As the work of schools continues to increase and intensify in the face of globalisation, migration, improvement, and national change agendas, "much more is being demanded of teachers by way of supporting and complementing the work of school leaders" (Miller, 2018, p. 85). They take on or take the lead in several areas, and as the demands on schools and teachers become even more complex, society expects schools to deal effectively with different languages and student backgrounds, to be sensitive to culture and gender issues, to promote tolerance and social cohesion, to respond effectively to disadvantaged students and students with learning or behavioural problems, to use new technologies, and to keep pace with rapidly developing fields of knowledge and approaches to student assessment (Organisation for Economic Co-operation and Development [OECD], 2005). Such demands place teachers not only at the centre of practice, but also at the forefront of leadership, devising, implementing, and leading change.

These demands are characteristic of changing national societies, and changing expectations of schools and schooling, not least because "school leadership is a collective endeavour that draws upon and makes use of all available talents and skills available in order to produce the best outcomes for students and for school" (Miller, 2018, p. 86), but because "all teachers must be educational leaders in order to optimize the teaching and learning experience for themselves and their students; and, as professionals, they are expected to do whatever it takes to make that happen" (Forster, 1997, p. 83). Teacher leaders "lead within and beyond the classroom...identify with and contribute to a community of teacher learners and leaders...and influence others towards improved educational practice" (Katzenmeyer & Moller, 2001, pp. 5–8). From this definition, it is to be observed that teachers are involved in both a moral and an ethical practice of leadership through leading learning, and through developing and working collaboratively with others. As well as being leaders in their own right, teachers are also agents of change. Miller (2016) described them as "mechanics" (p. 147), and later as, "the lifeblood of an education system, without whom, all the educational aims and objectives for society and for individuals may not be realised" (p. 79). Lipsky (1980) reaffirmed their importance, and indeed their important work by describing them as street level bureaucrats who establish and invent devices, decisions, and routines to cope with uncertainties and work pressure that become the public policies they carry out. Together these descriptions and characterisations underline the multi-functionality of a teacher's role not only in terms of teaching and learning, but also in terms of supporting and in providing leadership.

This multi-functional perspective of a teacher's role is appropriately captured in this book on teachers' work in the United States, England, and Jamaica. Through the accounts provided by participants in the studies undertaken by the authors, teachers are shown to be involved in problem solving, performance evaluation, safeguarding and improving standards, role modelling and capacity building, consulting and risk-taking, and in changing from the bottom-up. Although "only a limited number of teachers will pursue or receive opportunities to use all the skills they possess" (Miller, 2018, p. 85), it is crucial that teacher leadership is seen and regarded as highly intellectual work, where teachers assume responsibility for the learning of their students and for each other (Lieberman & Miller, 1992), and where a lot of skills are simultaneously used.

Teaching is a "moral practice" (Hansen, 2011, p. 4), and "scratch a good teacher and you will find a moral purpose" (Fullan, 1993, p. 2). The authors deserve commendations for surfacing apparent contradictions in the work of teachers, the conditions under which they work, and the role they play in leading class-based and school-based initiatives; analyses is made much more powerful and compelling through the critical, cross-cultural lens used to frame the discourse. Each country's data provides unique and perspectival insights into the context of teaching and leadership in each jurisdiction, and, as a whole, highlights and illuminates the field by adding to knowledge through both its content and its design and methodology.

References

Forster, E.M. (1997). Teacher leadership: Professional right and responsibility. *Action in Teacher Education, 19*(3), pp. 82-94. https://doi.org/10.1080/016266 20.1997.10462881

Fullan, M. (1993). Why teachers must become change agents. *Educational Leadership, 50*(6), 12–17.

Hansen, D. (2011) The Teacher and the World: A study of cosmopolitanism as education. Abingdon: Routledge.

Institute for Educational Leadership (2001). School leadership for the 21st century initiative: A report of the Task Force on Teacher Leadership, Washington, DC: IEL. Retrieved from http://www.s199986426.onlinehome.us/programs/21st/reports/teachlearn.pdf

Katzenmeyer, M., & Moller, G. (2001). *Awakening the sleeping giant: helping teachers develop as leaders.* Thousand Oaks, CA: Corwin Press.

Lieberman, A., & L. Miller. 1992. *Teachers, their world and their work: Implications for school improvement.* New York: Teachers College Press.

Lipsky, M. (1980). *Street-level bureaucracy: Dilemmas of the individual in public services.* New York: Russell Sage Foundation.

Maxey, C. (1956). The work of the teacher. *The Phi Delta Kappan,* 37(6), 264-266. Retrieved from http://www.jstor.org/stable/20341761

Miller, P. (2016). *Exploring school leadership in England and the Caribbean: New insights from a comparative approach,* London: Bloomsbury.

Miller, P. (2018). *The nature of school leadership: Global practice perspectives,* London: Palgrave Macmillan.

Organisation for Economic Co-operation and Development (OECD) (2005). *Teachers matter: Attracting, developing and retaining effective teachers (Overview),* Paris: OECD Publications.

INTRODUCTION

ELEANOR J. BLAIR, CARMEL ROOFE, SUSAN TIMMINS

If your actions inspire others to dream more, learn more, do more and become more, you are a leader.

—John Quincy Adams

A WILLINGNESS TO GRAPPLE with the complexities of teacher leadership and its impact—short- and long-term—on the profession is prerequisite to a meaningful consideration of how to make this phenomenon the norm rather than the exception among teachers. Although, it is important to remember that not all teachers want to be leaders and that many are currently happy with the status quo. Inherent to the concept of teacher leadership are many opportunities to change both the quantity and quality of teachers' work, but there has to be a willingness to go "there"; one has to be accepting of the risks and be enthusiastic about the work required to make it happen. Perhaps more challenging is the notion of change—major changes in how power and authority are negotiated and allocated among stakeholders in educational settings. Change may be the only constant we face, and yet, in many instances, it is the thing that causes massive waves of resistance and push-back from those involved. Thus, any consideration of teacher leadership must consider how to encourage, support, and nurture teacher leadership while simultaneously honoring the voices of those teachers (and administrators) who are not ready for change. As Phillip C. Schlechty (1993) argued in his essay, "On the frontier of school reform with trailblazers, pioneers, and settlers," we have to figure out what role we will play as change leaders within a school, but also, how we will deal with the saboteurs who are intent on stopping change at all costs. His final recommendation is worth considering:

Saboteurs can cause trouble, no matter where they are. But I have found that the best place to have them is on the inside where they can be watched rather than on the outside where they can cause trouble without its being detected until the effects are felt....If, however, change leaders continue to reach out to saboteurs and critics and try hard to hear what they are saying, sometimes there is much to be learned. (p. 50)

So, we have a vision—a vision about critical changes in the teaching profession, and more specifically, changes in the form of emergent teacher leadership that could potentially transform the lives and work of 21st-century teachers. We know what teacher leadership is theoretically; we also know what the current reality is for teachers working in contemporary schools. As a beginning, however, we ask you to consider how teacher leadership is discussed in the literature. The Center for Strengthening the Teaching Profession (CSTP, 2018) in their *Teacher Leadership Skills Framework* document asserts that:

In order for Teacher Leaders to flourish, certain characteristics and conditions must be present. Teacher Leaders must possess the knowledge and skills needed to lead. Consequently, to be seen as a leader, they must also have a set of positive dispositions and attitudes. Finally, there must be a variety of opportunities for leadership in the school, district or larger context. (p. 1)

They go on to suggest that teacher leaders have the following skills and dispositions:

1. Working with Adult Learners

2. Communication

3. Collaboration

4. Knowledge of Content and Pedagogy

5. Systems Thinking

6. Equity Lens (p. 1).

In conclusion, they describe teacher leaders as being unique in their possession of specific dispositions and attitudes: "They are energetic risk takers whose integrity, high efficacy, and content knowledge give them credibility with their colleagues. Their desire to work with adults is grounded in their belief that systems-level change will positively impact student learning, and that their contributions to the profession are important and needed" (Center for Strengthening the Teaching Profession, 2018, p. 1). Definitions of teacher leadership vary, but most are consistent in their inclusion of collaborative relationships within professional learning communities that support school improvement and high levels of professional efficacy. York-Barr and Duke (2004) provided a definition of teacher leadership that captured the most salient issues that emerged from their work:

> Teacher leadership is the process by which teachers, individually or collectively, influence their colleagues, principals, and other members of school communities to improve teaching and learning practices with the aim of increased student learning and achievement. Such leadership work involves three intentional development foci: individual development, collaboration or team development, and organizational development. (pp. 287–88)

Other notable authors have also attempted to define teacher leadership in the following ways:

> The term teacher leadership refers to that set of skills demonstrated by teachers who continue to teach students but also have an influence that extends beyond their own classrooms to others within their own school and elsewhere. It entails mobilizing and energizing others with the goal of improving the school's performance of its critical responsibilities related to teaching and learning. (Danielson, 2006, p. 12)

Action that transforms teaching and learning in a school, that ties school and community together on behalf of learning, and that advances social sustainability and quality of life for a community.... Teacher leadership facilitates principled action to achieve whole-school success. It applies the distinctive power of teaching to shape meaning for children, youth, and adults. And it contributes to long-term, enhanced quality of community life. (Crowther, Kaagen, Ferguson, & Hann, 2002, p. xvii)

When given opportunities to lead, teachers can influence school reform efforts. Waking this sleeping giant of teacher leadership has unlimited potential in making a real difference in the pace and depth of school change. (Katzenmeyer & Moller, 2001, p. 102)

More important to this discussion, however, is a consideration of the intersection of teacher leadership and the professional status of teachers. Efforts to raise the status of teaching have typically focused on three areas: licensing and training, compensation and working conditions, and finally, power, authority, and control over issues like curriculum, evaluation, and budgets (Lankford, Loeb, McEachin, Miller, & Wyckoff, 2014, pp. 444–45). When discussing teacher leadership and the professional status of teachers, issues of power, authority, and control over the context, process, and product of teachers' work come up over and over; teachers are often consulted or included in conversations *about* decision-making in these areas, but they are seldom given the authority to make decisions independently. For teachers choosing to remain in the profession and not advance to administration, there is no advancement within the profession that includes increased levels of responsibility, autonomy, and/or accountability. If teacher leadership in its broadest, most professional terms could be the norm, how would the teaching profession be transformed? Teacher leadership has the potential to do at least three things for teachers and the schools where they work:

- Teachers acting in leadership roles will automatically move the profession toward full professional status through a renewed emphasis on greater autonomy and decision-making within classrooms, schools, and the community. The working conditions at most schools would be transformed by the leadership of teachers.

- Teacher leaders will have more opportunities to negotiate roles and re-sponsibilities that may require extended days and/or school years in exchange for greater pay; however, these expanded roles and responsi-bilities will recognize and utilize the pedagogical knowledge and exper-tise of teachers.

- And finally, schools with high levels of teacher leadership will have greater levels of school improvement: e.g., higher test scores, profession-al learning communities that demonstrate high levels of collaboration, and cohesive curricular development and implementation. Overall, the school culture will be positively impacted by the growth of leadership capacity among all major stakeholders and in that way, school efficacy will increase (Acker-Hocevar & Touchton, 2011).

Research by Linda Lambert (2016) has documented that in schools where teachers function as both learner and leaders within professional learning communities (PLCs), we see the following:

- Supportive and Shared Leadership

- Shared Values and Vision

- Collective Learning and Application of Learning

- Supportive Conditions

- Shared Personal Practice

A key idea underlying much of Lambert's (1998) work on teacher leadership is the notion of leadership capacity building defined in the following way: "as an organizational concept meaning broad-based, skillful participation in the work of leadership that leads to lasting school improvement" (Lam-bert, 2005, para. 2). Building, nurturing, and facilitating leadership capacity enriches the ability of all major stakeholders to participate in an institution's capacity for broad-based participation in leadership activities; everyone has a voice and hierarchies become flat and leadership is distributed. As such, leadership capacity building provides opportunities to "grow" leaders from multiple layers of the organization. Within this context, we see the emergence of PLCs and ongoing leadership capacity building activities that yield higher levels of teacher satisfaction and school cultures that are engaged in the process of asking hard questions about practice and a willingness to research and seek out research-based answers that are relevant to different (and difficult) educational spaces. It is important for teachers (and administrators) to be mindful of the ways in which their work is seen and experienced by the larger community; a school program can be defined by the worst teachers working in isolation and in opposition to a collective vision. In these cases, damage in the form of student failure and a lack of collegiality occurs and impacts all stakeholders within the school and beyond. Often, the failures of bad teachers are publicly shared and delineated as if they are descriptive of all teachers in a school. Through collaboration, community building, and trust, teacher leaders can seek to deprivatize teaching and make public practice and sharing the norm. In this way, there are opportunities to expand teachers' work to include PLCs where the meaningful critique of pedagogical practice becomes the norm and the analysis of data and incorporation of research-based practices regularly leads to improved personal as well as group practice. In this way, teacher leadership can lead to school improvement in specific classrooms and across entire schools. More importantly, among teachers who are given opportunities and resources to be teacher leaders, the following outcomes are documented:

- Teacher Efficacy

- Retain Excellent Teachers

- Overcome Resistance to Change

- Career Enhancement

- Improve Own Performance

- Influence Other Teachers

- Accountability for Results (Katzenmeyer & Moller, 2001, pp. 32–34).

This process of unpacking prior assumptions and disrupting dominant narratives about pedagogy provides a context for professional growth and development. In this way, teachers and schools automatically begin to consider the philosophical as well as the structural changes necessary to move the teaching profession to a higher level of status and open the door for in-depth discussions regarding the ideological principles and frameworks that guide the advocacy work of teachers.

While it is a frequently accepted truth that principals have tremendous power to direct a school program and impact teachers, students, and the larger community, any administrator who ignores the untapped potential of teachers acting as leaders is, at best, unprepared, and perhaps, incompetent to lead a school. Teachers working in concert with a capable leader have opportunities to share leadership in ways that teachers working with authoritarian leaders do not. A quote from the Chinese philosopher, Lao Tzu, says it best: "A leader is best when people barely know he exists, when his work is done, his aim fulfilled, they will say: we did it ourselves" (Shinagel, n.d., para. 4). This quote exemplifies a relationship where leadership is a mutual process that requires respect and collaboration—a relationship where power and authority does not reside in an individual, but rather, in a shared accountability where responsibility and recognition for both successes and failures is "owned" by all stakeholders. Teachers acting as leaders have the power to be the provocateurs of front line dissent that leads to personal and professional transformation. In this way, teachers have opportunities to demonstrate their pedagogical expertise through a re-definition of the process and product of education within the context of diverse contemporary schools. The teaching profession would change; teachers would be granted a new level of respect and power as well as an opportunity to compete for the salaries and prestige granted to other educational leaders. And more importantly, overnight, schools would improve in meaningful and sustainable ways. How to bridge the gap between what is and what could be is the raison d'être for this work.

Stephen Covey (2013) in *The 7 Habits of Highly Effective People* suggests that "we have to begin with the end in mind." It is only by thinking about what teaching could be like if it had full professional status that we are thus able to envision what the road in that direction must look like—what must change, what must be discarded, and most importantly, what new provisions must be made. What would be a new image of 21st-century teachers? Unfortunately, the status quo for the teaching profession today is disappointing. The profession seems to have hit a proverbial wall; there is little growth in opportunities for teachers to assume new roles and responsibilities, and in so many present-day schools, there is a general frustration among teachers and a sense of hopelessness regarding the future of the profession. Thus, when thinking about the future of teacher leadership, a total reversal and transformation of the current mindset regarding school reform is necessary; clearly, we can't get there from here unless we begin to ask new questions and think about teachers and schools in new ways. It is much more than thinking out of the box; it is thinking out of buildings and classrooms and hierarchies that have traditionally defined how we structure and organize public education. How we define the problem does ultimately determine the solution. If we define the problems of the teaching profession as low test scores or as simply salary issues, we are doomed for failure. We can do a better job of teaching to the test and small increases in teacher salaries are inevitable, but real change, a change in the substance of the progress and product of teachers' work, will require a rethinking of what teachers do in schools and classrooms and how we assess the value of those tasks. If we begin with the end in mind, we have to envision what teacher leadership as the norm looks like in all of the different manifestations of teachers' work, and then we have to begin to think about how to make that happen. In this way, teachers' work and teachers' lives will change and a metamorphosis appropriate for 21st-century schools and education will occur.

Though the concept of leadership is contested in the literature and is often seen as occurring differently across cultures and contexts, as an organizational activity, leadership is seen as an activity which initiates change (Dimmock & Walker, 2002; Showunmi & Kaparou, 2017). Leadership for school improvement must be a system of participatory governance and decision-making existing as a community. Teachers based on the nature of their roles possess a great deal of power within schools that school leaders need to utilize for the benefit of all. As poignantly articulated by Lieberman and Miller (1999), "without teachers' full participation and leadership, any move to reform education no matter how well intentioned, is doomed to failure" (p. xi). An imperative therefore for better schools is for teachers to be given the opportunity to be involved in decision-making, especially those that affect them.

This book is perhaps the first to examine what teacher leadership looks like in three very different countries in the same volume: England, Jamaica, and the United States. In this book, while we provide insights from the three countries, we attempt to examine cross-cultural considerations in teachers' work through relying on the empirical evidence from 36 teacher leaders as we gleaned units of comparison across the three countries. In our cross-cultural considerations, for example, we created single-site matrices to explore each case separately and then created cross-site matrices to identify patterns across cases (Miles & Huberman, 1994). Additionally, as teacher educators working in three different country contexts, we have added our independent voices to the cross-cultural conversation through an informal conversation amongst us as authors. In attempting the cross-cultural conversation, we recognize that doing cross-cultural research is complex, hence, we have provided room for the reader to delineate his/her own comparisons through the detailed country cases we have provided.

In 1999, Michelle Acker-Hocevar and Debra Touchton published research conducted with six teacher leaders representing different parts of the state of Florida, in the United States. The teachers in Acker-Hocevar and Touchton's study sought to describe the decision-making structures, teacher culture, and power/micropolitics of the work of teachers who were selected as teacher of the year during the period of 1996 to 1997 (p. 2). Acker-Hocevar and Touchton discussed agency and power within the context of the social relationships within a school. They suggested that "responsibility and accountability may rest on the internal processes in the school to enable or 'empower' teachers to take a legitimate role in their school's development" (p. 3). Acker-Hocevar and Toughton used Clegg's 1989 work to discuss that by having a "working knowledge of the system and how to get around certain obstacles in the formal power structures, these teachers might affect change" (pp. 3–4). The research reported in this book sought to expand the earlier work of Acker-Hocevar and Touchton by focusing on three countries and emphasizing the personal, and very specific, perspectives of the geographical, physical, and social context for teachers' work. Additionally, we sought to focus on teachers who were identified as teacher leaders by their colleagues and not awarded as teachers of the year (See the methods section of each country case for a more detailed methodological explanation). The research was guided by two major areas of interest: first, how teachers describe the intersection of teachers' work, teacher leadership, and school culture, second, to expand the earlier work of Acker-Hocevar and Touchton to include the personal, and very specific, perspectives of teachers in cross-cultural settings. Teachers were asked to describe transformative teacher leadership and the role of advocacy in their work.

Across the three countries, we utilized the same kinds of questions used by Acker-Hocevar and Touchton in their study, as well as several questions that were unique to our project. In each country setting, teacher leaders were interviewed to capture how they describe their work, the intersection between teacher leadership and school culture, and how the role of power and advocacy functions in their work in 21st-century schools in unique settings. The interview provided a platform for the interviewees to "dig deeper" and examine personal beliefs and attitudes about teacher power and agency. The following are the questions that guided the research project.

1. Describe yourself as a teacher. How did you get here? Background? Education? Job experiences?

2. Describe the school culture where you work. Identify those people and things that support your work. Identify those people and things that make your job more difficult.

3. Do you consider yourself a Teacher Leader? Why or why not?

4. Describe the formal and informal processes that lead to decision making in your school. What roles do teachers play? Administrators? How people are held responsible/accountable for implementing decisions? What role do you play in decision making? How is this similar or different from other teachers?

5. How do you define teacher expertise? What is the teacher culture at your school for teachers to use their knowledge and expertise? How are various levels of expertise utilized? How does expertise afford your involvement in decision making?

6. Describe the power relationships within your school between different groups such as teachers and administrators. Probes for this question are: What do the teachers say about these relationships? How do you think about these relationships?

7. Tell us a story about how you use your personal power in school. Are advocacy or social justice issues a part of the work that you do? If so, give some examples. Help us gain "insights" into how or what you value and why it may be similar or different from other teachers or administrators.

Overall, the purpose of this research was to highlight personal narratives of power and agency in teachers' work and to identify the "lessons" that transcend individual circumstances and speak to the importance of understanding how teachers' work (and teacher leadership) functions within complex school cultures.

We believe that teacher leaders' work is key to efforts to improve schools and must be considered in ongoing school reform efforts. We therefore share this work as an attempt to give a voice to the concerns and issues expressed by teachers who are seldom recognized for their work in school improvement. It is our belief that the narratives shared by these teachers highlight the nested relationship between teachers' work, school culture, school leadership, power and agency, and school improvement.

The four sections in which the book is divided uniquely situate each author's findings within each country context while identifying the intersections across cultures and the "lessons" that transcend cultures. The general introduction to the book is an attempt to outline the scope, depth, and breadth of the topic as we explore the research, theory, and issues of praxis that intersect teachers' work in the three countries. Sections one, two, and three present our research on teacher leadership in England, Jamaica, and the United States. Within each of these sections, each author shares the relevant literature on teacher leadership in the specific country studied and simultaneously shares the unique aspects of the methodology and findings from this country. While highlighting both the similarities and differences across the countries, an informal conversation among the three authors in the final section (Section Four) presents a critical analysis of the status of teacher leadership as a global phenomenon. It is our hope that this book provides a context for the continuation of a much bigger conversation about teachers' work and the role of teacher leadership in advancing the teaching profession.

References

Acker-Hocevar, M. and Touchton, D. (1999). A Model of Power as Social Relationships: Teacher Leaders Describe the Phenomena of Effective Agency in Practice. Paper presented at the American Educational Research Association Annual Meeting, Montreal, Quebec, Canada. Retrieved from https://files.eric.ed.gov/fulltext/ED456108.pdf

Center for Strengthening the Teaching Profession (CSTP) (2018). Teacher leadership skills framework. Retrieved from http://www.cstp-wa.org

Covey, S. (2013). *The 7 habits of highly successful people: Powerful lessons in personal change* (Anniversary Edition). New York: Simon & Schuster.

Crowther, F., Kaagen, S. S., Ferguson, M., & Hann, L. (2002). *Developing teacher leaders: How teacher leadership enhances school success.* Thousand Oaks, CA: Corwin Press.

Danielson, C. (2006). *Teacher leadership that strengthen professional practice.* Alexandria, VA: ASCD.

Dimmock, C & Walker A. (2002). School leadership in context societal and organizational cultures. In T. Bush and L.Bell (Eds.), *The principles and practices of educational management* (pp.70–85). London. Sager. [AU: Please double check publisher]

Katzenmeyer, M. and Moller, G. (2001). *Awakening the sleeping giant: Helping teachers develop as leaders* (2nd Edition). Thousand Oakes, CA: Corwin Press.

Lambert, L. (1998). How to build leadership capacity. Educational Leadership, 55(7), 17–19.

Lambert, L. (2005, Spring). What does leadership capacity really mean? *Journal of Staff Development, 26*(2), 38–40. Retrieved from https://eric.ed.gov/?id=EJ752235

Lambert, L. (2016). *Liberating leadership capacity.* New York: Teachers College Press.

Lankford, H., Loeb, S., McEachin, A., Miller, L.C. and Wyckoff, J. (2014). Who enters teaching? Encouraging evidence that the status of teaching is improving. *Educational Researcher, 43*(9), 444–53.

Lieberman, A., & Miller, L. (1999). *Teachers—Transforming their world and their work.* New York: Teachers College Press.

Miles, M. B., & Huberman, A. M. (1984). *Qualitative data analysis.* London: Sage.

Schlechty, P. C. (1993, Fall). On the frontier of school reform with trailblazers, pioneers, and settlers. *Journal of Staff Development, 14*(4), 46–51.

Shinagel, M. (n.d.). The paradox of leadership. Harvard University, Harvard Extension School/Professional Development. Retrieved from https://www.extension.harvard.edu/professional-development/blog/paradox-leadership

Showunmi, V, & Kaparou, M. (2017). The challenge of leadership: ethnicity and gender Among school leaders in England, Malaysia, and Pakistan. In P. W. Miller (Eds.), *Cultures of educational leadership: global and intercultural perspectives,* pp. 95–119. Basingstoke, UK: Palgrave Macmillan.

York-Barr, J. and Duke, K. (2004, Autumn). What do we know about teacher leadership? Findings from two decades of scholarship. *Review of Educational Research, 74*(3), 255–316.

Teacher Leadership in England

CHAPTER ONE

Education in England

SUSAN TIMMINS

Introduction

THE EDUCATION SYSTEM IN England continues to face many challenges. Inadequate funding and resources, high staff turnover, teacher burnout, and a recruitment crisis are just a few areas highlighted by the National Education Union (NEU) and the Department for Education (DfE). There are a number of events happening in England currently which are impacting the effectiveness of whole school leadership; for example, the 'creation of educational markets', with 'high stakes accountability' through standards based testing, and monitoring of schools through inspections (Miller, 2016, p. 9). Increasingly, the government maintains control through punitive measures such as compulsory testing, targets, surveillance, and monitoring (Miller, 2016). All schools in England are held accountable and are regulated by the Office for Standards in Education, Children's Services and Skills (OFSTED). They inspect all services that provide education and skills for learners of all ages. OFSTED's role is to make sure that organizations who provide education, training, and care services do so to a high standard for children and students. Schools are inspected on average every three years and following an inspection are awarded an overall grade from the following scale: Grade 1: Outstanding, Grade 2: Good, Grade 3: Requires improvement, and Grade 4: Inadequate. OFSTED makes judgements across the following areas: effectiveness of leadership and management; quality of teaching, learning, and assessment; personal development, behavior, and welfare; and outcomes for pupils (OFSTED, 2018). As you can imagine, anything less than good or outstanding puts immense pressure on schools to improve.

Types of Schools in England

There are increasing numbers of different types of schools in England; the majority are either an academy or a maintained school. They differ in the way funding is allocated to the school and which organisation oversees them. Funding and oversight for maintained schools are provided by the local authority and most are classified as community schools, which means that the local authority employ the school's staff and are responsible for student admissions. Maintained schools in England are legally required to follow the statutory national curriculum, which sets out the programmes of study and the specific subject content for each subject that should be taught to all pupils.

Academies receive their funding and are overseen by the Department for Education (DfE) via the Education and Skills Funding Agency. They are also run by an academy trust which employs the staff. Academies do not have to follow the National Curriculum but are required to deliver a 'broad and balanced' curriculum which includes English, mathematics, science, and religious education. Children in academies have to sit for national tests, so for this reason, many academies do choose to follow the national curriculum.

Two types of academies have evolved; a convertor academy (those deemed by OFSTED to be performing well that have converted to academy status) and sponsored academies (in the main, underperforming schools changing to academy status and run by sponsors). On comparison of the most recent OFSTED grades, convertor academies are most likely to be good or outstanding while sponsored academies are more likely than maintained schools to be graded, require improvement or are inadequate. This is not surprising, as convertors were high performing to start with and sponsored low performing, hence the prompted move to academy status to support school improvement. Many academies are part of an academy chain or multi-academy trust, which means that they can benefit from economies of scale for services and resources that they need, and therefore more money can be spent per pupil. The government appears to be more in favour of academies and hold the view that they drive up standards and hold the belief that schools converting to academy status sets them free from the bureaucracy of the local authorities (Rosen, 2016).

Critics of academies Lucy Powell (2016), a former shadow education secretary, and Kevin Courtney, deputy general secretary for the National Union of Teachers (NUT), claim that academy status does not result in higher attainment or in fact lead to school improvement. Furthermore, they suggest that many academies are in fact failing their pupils, particularly their disadvantaged pupils. OFSTED claims that whilst there can be clear benefits to becoming an academy, there is little difference performance-wise between academies and those schools maintained by local authorities (2016).

The diversity of England's school system continues to grow, and irrespective of whether a school is an academy or a maintained school, the quality of the school is contingent on attracting and retaining the best teachers and leaders. During inspections in 2014, OFSTED highlighted that leadership was not good enough at a staggering 3,500 schools, and of those, a disproportionately high number of secondary schools were identified where leadership was judged to be inadequate or required improvement.

The State of Education

According to Monteiro (2015), 'There have been a range of international and national reports and studies proclaiming that the overall status of the teaching profession is not very prestigious' and refers to 'decline' and 'lack of recognition' as two terms frequently associated to the status of the teaching profession worldwide (p. 61). In 1997 a report compiled jointly by the International Labour Organization (ILO) and the United Nations Educational, Scientific and Cultural Organization (UNESCO), Committee of Experts observed that in virtually every country reported upon, the status of teachers when compared with other professions was low or, in some instances, had actually deteriorated in recent years. Fast forward to 2019 and the picture is not much improved in England, with teacher remuneration and status comparing unfavourably with other professions, fewer entrants to the profession, and retention of teachers at an all-time low. According to the National Foundation for Educational Research (Worth and Van den Brande, 2019), the number of working-age teachers leaving the profession has increased from 25,000 in 2010–11 to 36,000 in 2016–17. They found that whilst 85% of early career teachers remained in the profession at the end of their first year, the three-year retention rate dropped from 80% to 73% in 2017. What is worse, the five-year retention rate has dropped from 73% in 2011 to 67% in 2017.

The National Education Union (NEU) (2019) criticized the government for being slow to respond to the teacher recruitment and retention crisis and further maintain that the situation is worsening:

> Work life balance is worse than a year ago, and the linked issues of workload and accountability are the main reasons education professionals don't see themselves working in the sector in the near future. (p. 1)

The NEU gathered views from 8,000 teachers, school leaders, and support staff from across the United Kingdom (UK) on the State of Education and the conditions they have to work under. Regrettably, 40% of the respondents foresee that they will no longer be working in education by 2024, and a staggering 18% expect to be gone within two years. What appears to be emerging, and should be a major concern to government, is the declining retention rate of recently qualified teachers. The same survey found similar alarming results:

- Twenty-six percent of those with between 2–5 years' experience intend to leave education in the next five years.

- For those with less than 2 years' experience, this drops to a still significant 15%.

Workload and accountability were the main reasons offered for why teachers would choose to leave the profession.

> *'My job is no longer about children. It's just a 60-hour week with pressure to push children's achievement data through'.* (p. 1)

'*Exhausted and fed up with the hours I have to maintain in order to keep abreast of paperwork demands. I love the teaching but have grown tired of how relentless the job has become*'. (p. 1)

Many staff surveyed raised the issues of being micro-managed, and when asked how their job could be improved, they responded:

'*To be trusted more as a professional and scrutinised less. The amount of monitoring in our school is excessive*'. (p. 1)

The NEU report stated that teachers felt that the workload in schools would not diminish until the accountability regime is relinquished and schools become more balanced and more focused on teaching and supporting children, rather than committing valuable resources towards damaging factors such as teaching to the test, focusing on tasks, paperwork, and data analysis for inspectors.

In an attempt to resolve the teacher retention and recruitment crisis in England, the Department for Education (DfE) launched a new strategy in January 2019 which seeks to attract more people to the profession and encourage those who are in the classroom to stay. The main focus of the strategy is on early career support, flexible hours, reducing workload, and simplifying the process of application to teacher training programs. The most substantial change could be through the creation of an Early Career Framework (ECF), which guarantees a 5% reduction in teaching load during the second year of teaching. Presently, newly qualified teachers get 10% reduction in the first year and no reduction in the second year. In addition, they are committed to ensuring that teachers have access to curriculum and training materials, and funding for mentors to support early career teachers (Department for Education, 2019). It could be argued that this is a step in the right direction compared to existing strategies such as teacher bursaries, more familiarly known in the United States as scholarships. Bursaries are designed to attract teachers to the profession; however, focusing on financial incentives can often attract individuals who are not really dedicated to becoming teachers and have no real desire to do it in the long term. They can often view the training year as a year out of their normal profession, or a 'filling-in' year before they go on to do what they really want to do. As a teacher educator, I have witnessed this on a number of occasions whereby trainees have received a £26,000 tax free bursary whilst they are training to be a teacher and then after a year, they decide against becoming a teacher. Sometimes, after completing their training, they return to their previous jobs or go on to do something else. Whilst this is particularly frustrating on my part as a teacher educator, it is even more so felt by the school mentors who have dedicated so much time, effort, and support to help develop the trainees' teaching practices and enable them to qualify as secondary school teachers.

The Department for Education (DfE) has done very little to raise the profile of the teaching profession. Their strategy has been heavily focused around recruiting newcomers to the profession rather than retaining valuable teachers who are already in the profession. The recent focus on reducing workload, developing formal leadership roles, and renewing emphasis on health and well-being for teachers can be seen as an attempt to persuade teachers to remain or persuade others to join. However, they have not given sufficient thought as to how as a society, we build respect for teachers as professionals and convey trust that they will do a good job of educating children.

> Giving teachers' responsibility as professionals and leaders of reform, and trusting their professional responsibility, is the greatest challenge to reform. (Organisation for Economic Co-operation and Development, 2011, p. 5)

However, many would argue that increased government intervention is fast becoming counter-productive. Bassey (2005) asserts that whenever there is a change in political party, ministers are keen to introduce their new 'pet scheme' and draw up new league tables and curriculums and tests. Bassey goes on to say:

> It is time to stop: day by day it is teachers who know best what their pupils need. It is time for government to trust teachers and to

transfer to them the power to exercise that trust in the best interest
of the pupils and parents whom they serve. (p. 7)

The government is also keen to promote every teacher as a researcher,
and whilst I agree that educational research is the most durable way of ensuring high-quality learning and teaching, the government has not removed
any existing pressures for teachers such as inspections, targets, external
tests, or league tables. All of which are tasks that reduce the time, energy,
and courage teachers need to participate in research and scholarship work.
It is only when these burdens have disappeared or have been adjusted that
research will have a much greater role in teachers' work.

Embracing and utilizing the skills of teacher leaders within our schools
is an important step forward that is prerequisite to steering us through these
challenges. Teacher leaders exist within our school organisations, and tapping into this important resource is an absolute must! Valuing this potential
and placing trust in these professionals can capture teacher leaders' abilities
and potential and positively impact whole school improvement that benefits
all students.

Teacher Leadership

Effective leadership is commonly accepted as being an essential component in acquiring and sustaining school improvement. Indications from the
school improvement literature repeatedly highlight how effective leaders can
employ an indirect power and influence on a school's ability to improve as a
school organisation and improve outcomes for students (Earley et al., 2012).
Whilst it is recognized that senior managers can be the main influencers, it
is accepted that the power of middle level leaders and teachers can also be a
key asset. Harris (2004), Leithwood and Riehl (2003) describe how teacher
leaders 'rally round' and work with others towards shared goals. In fact,
much of the evidence advocates that teacher leadership is greatest in collaborative settings and where there is a culture of trust (Caine, 2000; Little,
2000). This aligns with Gronn's (2000) conception of leadership as 'fluid
and emergent' rather than 'fixed' and which has greatest effect when it is a
shared activity (p. 333) Whilst Muijs and Harris (2006) would confer that

collaboration is necessary for teacher leadership, they extend the discourse on teacher leadership by presenting its close connection with distributed leadership claiming that it is:

> Conceptually narrower, being concerned exclusively with the leadership roles of teaching staff, while simultaneously being broader than many practical operationalization's of distributed leadership that have often concentrated on formal positional roles, in particular those relating to middle management and subject leadership. (p. 962)

Whilst the majority of the literature highlights the favorable effects of teacher leadership upon schools and students, there is little research that has explored the characteristics and influence of teacher leadership within schools in England. Miller (2018) notes that demands from changing government policy have caused changes to the structures of schools, which in turn has affected the way schools are led and managed. Furthermore, these changes are contributing to a 'dismantling of heroic leadership tendencies' (p. 91). Heroic leaders are perceived as self-centered individuals leading organisations, often individualists who make decisions without consulting colleagues. Recognising teachers as leaders in education and in school leadership is not only practical, but a necessary juxtaposition that pushes back against heroic or solo leadership approaches. Little (2003) suggests that conflict over the meaning of teacher leadership and designations applied such as 'intensification of labour' or an 'expanded' role for teachers as suggested by Ballett and Kelchtermans and Hargreaves, (as cited in Lee-Piggott, 2014, p. 107) are a large part of the problem. Bascia argues that these 'expanded concepts of teachers' work should not be classified as teacher leadership (as cited in Lee-Piggott, 2014, p. 107). Rather, these additional duties and responsibilities should be viewed as things that take away valuable time that could be committed to school improvement through activities that intersect with the professional training, growth, and development of teachers.

Prior to this study, further consideration was given to establishing how teacher leadership is defined, and more specifically, what do teacher leaders actually do? There are many definitions that define a teacher leader, such as 'someone who works with colleagues for the purpose of improving teaching and learning in a formal or informal capacity' (Patterson and Patterson, 2004, p. 74) Lee-Piggott (2014) identified both formal teacher leaders and informal teacher leaders as contributing to the goals of overall school improvement. Formal teacher leaders would include heads of departments, senior teachers, or curriculum leaders, whereas a less formal teacher leader undertakes a leadership role that is irrespective of position or delegation (p. 109). Bascia denotes this type of teacher leadership as 'invisible' (Bascia, 1997 as cited in Lee-Piggott, 2014, p. 109). Frost and Durrant (2003) stress that the term 'informal' should not be interpreted as the lack of a formal position, but more as a teacher elected to contribute to school improvement. Danielson (2007) perceives informal teacher leaders as 'emerging spontaneously and organically from the teacher ranks', further suggesting that 'teacher leaders are respected for their own teaching capabilities by fellow teachers' (p. 16). As such, definitions of teacher leadership vary with regard to how both formal and informal leadership roles are integrated into conceptions of teachers' work, but nevertheless, the significance and potential of these contributions are not challenged. Teacher leadership is a notion that has sustained many different manifestations, and yet it persists as an important component of school improvement. Wasley (1991) provided further insight into teacher leadership and highlighted some of the skills and qualities that they may possess:

> Teacher leaders are recognized by their peers and administrators as those staff members who are always volunteering to head new projects, mentoring and supporting other teachers, accepting responsibility for their own professional growth, introducing new ideas, and promoting the mission of the school. (p. 112)

Linda Lambert (2003) offered a broader definition of a teacher leader, as 'a person in whom the dream of making a difference has been kept alive, or has been reawakened by engaging colleagues and a professional culture' (p. 422). They are perceived as extremely skilled individuals, with a strong sense of justice and high expectations of students. With a strong commitment to school improvement and developing teaching and learning, they are influencers and can do this in a formal or informal capacity. Neito (2007) also claims that teacher leaders have high expectations of their fellow teachers and students. They often question and challenge the norm while simultaneously modeling principles of social justice. Most importantly, they use their influence inside and outside the classroom. Others portray similar definitions of a teacher leader as someone 'who leads within and beyond the walls of the classroom' (Katzenmeyer & Moller, 2009, p. 6).

An important component of this discussion is the belief that in order for teacher leaders to be successful, they need to operate in the right context or school culture that supports and facilitates their work as teacher leaders. As Muijs and Harris (2006) suggest, school leaders need to establish systems and provide encouraging and supportive conditions for the sharing of leadership (p. 967). Furthermore, senior leaders (head teachers, senior management teams, and governors) must lead effectively by establishing policies and processes that reflect an authentic commitment to developing shared leadership, creativity, and innovation.

It is apparent from a review of the literature that schools in England are not developing leadership capacity to its fullest potential and they are, in fact, missing a 'trick' by not tapping into the rich resource that exists in the form of teacher leadership, which exists within all school organizations. I suspect that many head teachers continue to have the mindset that people are either leaders or they are not, and leadership is not something that can be developed. However, the literature suggests that all teachers have the right, capability, and responsibility to be leaders. The challenge for senior leaders is to create the right conditions that evoke opportunities in which teacher leaders can lead and facilitate the leadership capacity of the organisation. What is more, Senior Management Teams (SMTs) that include principals, assistant principals, and others in formal leadership positions that guide and govern teachers need to work towards creating professional learning communities, as this, according to Lambert (1998), is at the heart of a high leadership capacity school. 'They are parallel constructs' (p. 426).

References

Bassey. M. (2005). *Teachers and government a history of intervention in education.* London: The Association of Teachers and Lecturers. Retrieved from https:// www.atl.org.uk/Images/Teachers%20and%20government.pdf

Caine, G., & Caine, R.N. (2000). The learning community as a foundation for developing teacher leaders. *NASSP Bulletin, 616*(84), 7–14. https://doi.org/10.1177/ 019263650008461603

Danielson, C. (2006). *Teacher leadership that strengthens professional practice*, Alexandria, VA: Association for Supervision & Curriculum Development. Retrieved from http://ebookcentral.proquest.com/lib/hud/detail.action?docID =3002154

Danielson, C. (2007). The many faces of leadership. *Educational Leadership, 65*(1), 14–19.

Department for Education (2019). *Teacher recruitment and retention strategy*. Retrieved from https://assets.publishing.service.gov.uk/government/uploads/ system/uploads/attachment_data/file/786856/DFE_Teacher_Retention_Strategy_ Report.pdf

Earley, P., Higham, R., Allen, R., Allen, T., Howson, J., Nelson, R., Rawar, S., Lynch, S., Morton, L., Mehta, P., & Sims, D. (2012). *Review of the school leadership landscape*. Retrieved from http://www.lcll.org.England/uploads/ 3/0/9/3/3093873/ review_of_school_leadership_landscape_2012_dec.pdf

Frost, D., & Durrant, J. (2003). *Teacher-led development work: Guidance and support*. London, UK: David Fulton.

Gronn, P. (2000). Distributed properties: A new architecture for leadership. *Educational Management Administration & Leadership, 28*(3), 317–338. https:// doi.org/10.1177/0263211X000283006

Harris, A. (2004). Distributed leadership and school improvement: Leading or misleading? *Educational Management & Administration 32*(1), 11–24.

International Labour Organisation (1997). Recommendation concerning the status of higher-education teaching personnel. Retrieved from http://portal.unesco.org/ en/ev.php-URL_ID=13144&URL_DO=DO_TOPIC&URL_SECTION=201. html

Katzenmeyer, M., & Moller, G. (2009). Helping teachers develop as leaders. Thousand Oaks, California: Corwin.

Lambert, L. (1998). *Building leadership capacity in schools*, Alexandria, VA: Association for Supervision and Curriculum Development.

Lambert, L. (2003). Leadership redefined: An evocative context for teacher leadership. *School Leadership & Management, 23*(4), 421–430. https://doi.org/10.1080/ 1363243032000150953

Lee-Piggott, R. (2014). When teachers lead: An analysis of teacher leadership in one primary school. *Caribbean Curriculum, 22*, 105–132.

Leithwood, K., & Riehl, C. (2003). "What do we already know about successful school leadership?" Paper presented at the annual meeting of the American Educational Research Association, Chicago, IL.

Little, J.W. (2000). Assessing the prospects for teacher leadership. In *The Jossey-Bass reader on educational leadership* (390–419). Chicago, IL: Jossey-Bass

Miller. P, (2016). *Exploring school leadership in England and the Caribbean: New insights from a comparative approach*. London: Bloomsbury.

Miller, P.W. (2018). *The nature of school leadership: Global practice perspectives*. UK: Palgrave Macmillan. Retrieved from http://ebookcentral.proquest.com

Monteiro A.R. (2015). *The teaching profession*. Springer Briefs in Education. Cham; Heidelberg: Springer.

Muijs, D., & Harris, A. (2006). Teacher led school improvement: Teacher leadership in the UK. *Teaching and Teacher Education, 22*(8), 961–972. https://doi.org/ 10.1016/j.tate.2006.04.010

National Education Union. (2019). *The state of education: Workload*. Retrieved from https://neu.org.uk/press-releases/state-education-workload

Neito, S. (2007). The colour of innovative and sustainable leadership: Learning from teacher leaders. *Journal of Educational Change, 8*(4), 299–309. https://doi. org/ 10.1007/s10833-007-9044-8

OFSTED (2016). *The Annual Report of Her Majesty's Chief Inspector of Education, Children's Services and Skills 2016/17*. Retrieved from https://assets. publishing.service.gov.uk/government/uploads/system/uploads/attach- ment_data/file/666871/Ofsted_ Annual_Report_2016-17_Accessible.pdf

OFSTED (2018). *School Inspection Handbook*. (150066). Retrieved from https:// assets.publishing.service.gov.uk/government/uploads/system/uploads/attach- ment_data/file/730127/School_inspection_handbook_section_5_270718.pdf

Organisation for Economic Co-operation and Development (2011). *Education at a Glance 2011 OECD indicators*. Retrieved from https://www.oecd.org/education/ skills-beyond-school/48631582.pdf

Patterson, J., & Patterson, J. (2004). Sharing the lead. *Educational Leadership, 61*(7), 74–78. Retrieved from http://educationalleader.com/subtopicintro/ read/ASCD/ASCD_237_1.pdf

Powell, L., & Courtney, K. (2016). *National Union of Teachers*. Retrieved from https://www.teachers.org.uk/news-events/press-releases-england/academies- and-league-tables

Rosen, M. (2016, March 20-3). Michael Rosen on academy schools: 'Local democracy bites the dust.' *The Guardian*. Retrieved from https://www.theguardian.com/ education/2016/mar/20/michael-rosen-on-academy-schools-local-democracy- bites-the-dust

Wasley, P.A. (1991) *Teachers who lead: The rhetoric of reform and the realities of practice*. New York: Teachers College Press.

Worth, J. & Brande, J. (2019). Teacher labour market in England: Annual report 2019. Retrieved from https://www.nfer.ac.uk/teacher-labour-market-in-england- annual-report-2019/

CHAPTER TWO

The Study of Teacher Leaders in England and Their Work

SUSAN TIMMINS

FOR THE PURPOSE OF this research, the intention was to identify teacher leaders who were not defined by a specific formal role or accountability (e.g., that of an assistant head or subject leader). The aim was to identify individuals who associated with a more informal teacher leader role and those who were perceived by others as leaders because they displayed a certain set of 'teacher leadership' behaviours, skills and qualities, such as those discussed above. This, however, was quite challenging, as I found that the majority of teachers who were recommended by others had already taken on teaching and learning responsibilities (TLRs) or formal management roles and were receiving remuneration for this. What I discovered was that in an effort to retain good staff, in most of the cases, the senior management team (SMT) in schools had encouraged teachers to take on additional responsibilities and promoted them really quickly. In some cases, teachers had taken on responsibilities in their second year of teaching, after successful completion of their newly qualified teacher (NQT) year.

Methodology

Twelve participants took part in this research. The teachers were employed at either an academy or state-maintained secondary school in the north of

England. An equal division of schools and academies were involved in this research and the schools were graded by OFSTED between Grade 1: Outstanding to Grade 3: Requires Improvement. The participants also varied in their range of experiences as teachers in secondary school settings. A summary of teacher, school demographic and OFSTED grading is found in Table 2.1.

Table 2.1: Teacher, School Demographics and OFSTED Grading

Teacher	Teaching experience (Years)	Type of school	Rural/Urban	OFSTED Grading
Isla	11	A	U	O
Diane	5	A	R	RI
Alexis	19	S	R	G
Harry	4	S	U	I
Kelly	4	A	U	O
Peter	2	A	R	O
Karl	9	A	U	O
Lucy	14	A	U	RI
Max	1	S	U	O
Elaine	8	A	R	O
Sam	3	S	R	RI
Jo	5	S	U	RI

A = Academy, S = State School, U = Urban, R = Rural
O = Outstanding, G = Good, RI = Requires Improvement, I = Inadequate

However, Lambert (2003a) asserts that teachers' ability to lead is dependent on the right context, and this must exist for their actions to have influence (p. 421). Teacher leadership demands a redistribution of power, a diffusion of power away from the head teacher to other educators within the school. However, Anderson (2011) questions whether this disseminated nature of leadership is truly empowering for teachers or simply a redistribution of work, with little or no increase in power or influence. As head of department, Harry felt powerless to influence change at a whole school level, but empowered to make decisions at a departmental level:

It's deemed that a non-leadership teacher has no power, whereas SMTs do have power to make changes at a whole school level. The teachers have the power to change things in their classroom, but not outside of this. All the politics, the policies, the changes that are made is not done by teachers. The changes are done by a handful of maybe non-teaching members of the governing body, or SMT, but it's certainly not done collectively. (Harry)

Max also felt that he had influence at a departmental level, but not at whole school level:

I'd like to think that I have an element of say in the decision making. When decisions come down to me, I feel that I can't make any great difference. I do like to think that I can make my point and ask if it could be raised or taken back to SMT. By doing this, I feel optimistic that I can influence some kind of change. (Max)

An interesting analogy by Max: 'when decisions come down to me', suggests a top-down approach on school decision-making. Lucy felt that influence and power had to be earned; it was not something that you walked into a school and demanded. This power was earned through the success of her subject and student outcomes:

For me, I don't think I have any power, but I do think I can influence things creatively. When I got here, I got really good results for three years. I made an impact with the school show and everything we did; I felt like it turned to gold. (Lucy)

Many department heads and department members draw their sense of self through their membership in their department (Clarke, 2013, p. 1226). This positioning shapes 'social identity, professional community and the social organization of the school' (Sisken & Little, 1995, p. 8). For these teachers, the focus is very much on their individual subject areas. Clark (2013) suggests that the subject can be used as a filter and therefore prevent an individual's ability to participate in whole school decision-making. Comments from both Lucy and Max might suggest a form of balkanization, which aligns with ideas from Hargreaves and Fullan (1998) and Acker-Hocevar and Touchton (1999), who suggest that balkanization has detrimental effects on school culture. This was the case at Diane's school after a recent OFSTED visit. The school had been graded 'Requires Improvement' from an OFSTED inspection; the poor grading category was mainly down to poor leadership and management. As a result of this, a new senior management team had been put in place. Diane spoke of divisions between 'old staff and new staff' and how this had a negative influence on the school culture:

> The staff culture here is not great! There are some staff who do get on and are quite supportive, but there is conflict between 'old staff' and 'new staff'. Sometimes, in a big meeting someone in SMT will refer to 'how it used to be' or say 'if we go back three years'. Usually they will say something quite derogatory about the school life in general, and the 'older' staff will take offence and say 'actually it was fine!' I am sure there was a point when it as actually fine, but tensions do exist. (Diane)

It is commonplace when schools have been graded 'Inadequate' or 'Requires Improvement' by OFSTED, that there is a change of leadership within the school. As in Diane's situation, some staff felt that this new senior management team had come in to 'sort them out' and this led to some teachers isolating themselves, and created a negative 'individualism teacher culture' (Acker-Hocevar & Touchton, 1999). This is where teachers withdraw from threatening, unpleasant situations and isolate themselves from the SMT and whole school activities, because they don't feel appreciated. To protect themselves from feelings of disempowerment, teachers do not get involved in collaborative working and decision-making, and this then results in disunion of culture.

Generally, many teacher leaders felt that they didn't really have sufficient power to influence whole school decisions. One teacher leader suggested that power and influence had to be earned, through successfully leading a department, or consistently achieving good student outcomes. Often, feelings of powerlessness caused 'divisions' in the staffroom, between those who had been at the school for many years and newer staff, who had come to the school and had been promoted through the ranks quite quickly. It was surprising to observe a general acceptance of the overall power being held by the senior management in the organisation. Max's description of the decision-making, 'when decisions come down to me' (meaning a whole school decision) expresses that acceptance of the distribution of power quite clearly.

Decision-making structures

Pellicer et al., (1990) found that, in the most effective schools, instructional leadership is a shared responsibility of teachers and head teachers. Similarly Rosenholz (1989) and Sickler (1988) reported positive effects when teachers were involved in the decision-making in schools, and the transformation of school organisations. Further studies (Leithwood & Jantzi, 1999; Helm, 1989) suggest a variety of ways that teachers can participate in decision-making and lead school development. These include: allowing staff to manage their own decision-making committees, using staff voice, providing independence for teachers and shared decision-making. Furthermore, they suggested adjusting working conditions so that staff have collaborative planning time, and opportunities to take part in staff development. Whilst it is recognised that instigating whole school reform moves more slowly where the leadership is shared with teachers, it is more commonly accepted and executed well (Weiss & Cambone, 2000).

Isla works as a lead teacher in an academy graded 'Outstanding' by OFSTED; she felt that the SMT had taken positive steps to enable shared decision-making across the school.

> I think the decisions are made collectively here and include the ideas
> of students and certainly the views of staff. (Isla)

She also describes a new layer of lead teachers that have been put in place by the academy:

> SMT work very closely with the lead teachers. They are the teaching
> and learning hub of the school and they carry out a lot of learning
> walks. There are ten lead teachers and they are paid extra for carry-
> ing out this role. The lead teachers are responsible for different ele-
> ments such as pupil premium or teacher training. All lead teachers
> meet with the vice principal to feedback ideas, conversations they
> have had with teachers and notes from observations. Lead teachers
> therefore, do have a large input into whole school decision-making.
> Whilst all decisions continue to go via SMT, staff can still give their
> ideas. SMT meet lead teachers on a weekly basis; they are very keen
> to keep on top of the different processes, any new initiatives and
> staff voice. (Isla)

Here, we can observe a deliberate effort by the SMT to initiate conditions
and empower staff, as they introduce a new layer of lead teachers in the
academy. Even though these are a formalised leader role, it is, I believe,
a step in the right direction. It is a deliberate attempt to share the decision-making which can then shape the future development of the school.
Muijs and Harris (2003), however, propose that leadership roles cannot
successfully be imposed by management. Walsey (1991) reiterates and states
that teachers need to be involved in the process of deciding what role, if
any, they wish to take on. Karl, a curriculum lead at the same academy, had
slightly different perceptions of the decision-making structure.

> As curriculum leaders, we have meetings at set times of the year and
> normally things will be unveiled at those meetings by SMT. We then
> have a chance to discuss the decisions and we filter them down to
> our teams. Sometimes meetings with SMT are two way, and some-
> times it is literally, 'This is what is happening; make it happen!' I
> don't always agree with the decisions. (Karl)

Individuals' perceptions of the decision-making structure within the school
appeared dependent on their role within the school. Isla felt empowered as
a lead teacher and believed that she could influence whole school improve-

ment. Furthermore, she felt that her voice was heard and she could speak on behalf of other teachers. Karl, on the other hand, experienced a mix of approaches. Sometimes initiatives were 'unveiled' and he just had to do it and accept things. Other times, Karl felt that he could contribute to the decision-making. Ultimately, it depended upon what the decision was being made about.

We could deduce here that the academy is taking positive steps by including staff in the decision-making structures, albeit in a formal manner. Acker-Hocevar and Touchton (1999), however, would suggest that this could be perceived as contrived. When 'teachers are told what to implement' and collaboration among teachers is not spontaneous, the outcomes are 'predictable rather than unpredictable'. Furthermore, they suggest that teachers may be 'cosmetically empowered' by schools when they give the impression that they are collaborative, but in reality, they are not. (Hargreaves, 1994, cited in Acker -Hocevar & Touchton, 1999, p. 15). Lucy discussed a situation where she felt consulted and she contributed to the decision-making in an informal way.

The other day the head came to me and said, 'I would like to run the idea of "quiet corridor" R with you. What do you think?' I thought that this was a good idea, especially for the areas in the school which are open plan and when students are moving from room to room; it would be great if they were quiet. A few years ago, that decision would have just happened, and in the morning briefing, SMT would have announced that this is what we are doing. There has definitely been a shift towards trying to include all staff in the decision-making and SMT are more approachable. (Lucy)

Diane, Harry and Peter all had very similar experiences; they worked in state-maintained secondary schools which had been graded 'Requires Improvement' by OFSTED. A school which is graded less than good operates under immense pressure. Staff, at all levels, can experience high levels of stress. Furthermore, a poor grading can greatly influence the style of leadership adopted by the SMT, and which staff are included in the decision-making process. Some teacher leaders interviewed, described individuals within the senior management team, who wanted to be seen to make a difference quickly. Sometimes the decisions they made were seen to be purely for their own gains or as an opportunity to fast-track to senior management positions:

> Teachers are not involved a lot in the decision-making; I think this is quite a negative aspect of this school. To be honest, I think that many decisions get made in small meetings made up of SMT members and without staff. Things get told to us all the time and there is never an opportunity to give our opinion before decisions are made. We are not consulted. (Peter)

> I was asked to be in a sort of focus group two years ago and I went for a short time. It was linked with teaching and learning and we discussed how we were going to promote challenge in school. However, because I strongly disagreed with something, it was just like 'well this is what we are going to do anyway' so, I kind of just stopped going. (Laugh). I thought, 'So what's the point!' It's not really a focus group it's just something like a 'token gesture'. (Diane)

> From my position, I have no say in the decision-making at all! Everything is done by SMT or governors. There has been no communication with middle leaders such as 'we are proposing this what do you think?' Now that did happen when previous SMT were involved, but now it is not happening. It's very much a top-down approach. (Harry)

> I am not involved in whole school decisions! I am allowed to make departmental decisions. From a whole school perspective, it's very much; you have a say but there are no real benefits of having that say, because nothing is ever changed. So, it's like a token gesture; they ask for your input but nothing is ever done with it, or it doesn't appear that things are done with it. On the whole, I feel that whole school decisions are made by a small handful of SMT without any consultation at all. (Peter)

The teachers articulated how they see themselves and others in the decision-making structures. Some teachers felt that they were exerting agency through voice at a departmental level, but had very little influence at a whole school level. Diane wanted to engage in collaborative decision-making, however, she quickly realised that things were contrived, and it was not truly an opportunity for agency and voice. Introducing new layers of lead teachers within academies is undoubtedly a very positive step forward and could result in opportunities for teachers to be involved in the overall decision-making structure. However, it is questionable as to whether this is some form of cosmetic empowerment, and is it just for show? Time will tell. On reflection, it was apparent that when teachers feel that they make a difference, they are involved and dedicated; where there is little or no impact, there is passiveness and acceptance.

Steering through the politics

Bacharach (1983) describes schools as political systems, whereby members are considered political players with their own needs, objectives and approaches to achieve those objectives (p. 10). Different perceptions can be held by those groups, with regard to who has the informal power (influence), or who they think should have the power to make the organisational decisions. 'Power, conflict, coalitions and policy are alive and well in schools' (Owen, 2006 cited in Brosky, 2011, p. 2). Owen further asserts that much of the time education is not about what is best for children; it is about the adult issues of power and control (p. 3). Blase and Anderson (1995) recognise that teachers are not inactive in the politics of the school; they do in fact, deploy a range of strategies to increase negotiating power through utilising influence tactics. In this study, the teacher leaders described the positive and negative forms of power and influence in the schools within which they worked. They acknowledged the positive influencing actions of teachers such as: approachability, offering advice, respect and trust, support of the school culture and building relationships. They also recognized the negative influences such as unhealthy alliances amongst colleagues, leaders who influence negatively and individuals who influence to advance their own personal agenda.

Karl felt that senior leaders should be perceived as holding a position of power; he felt that the power displayed by the SMT was a positive influence in his school. He also described the SMT as having a positive 'presence'.

> I think senior leaders have a certain presence, especially at this school; everyone knows who they are. SMT are out on the corridors supporting staff, they don't lock themselves in an office, and they are out on the corridors every change over, lunch time and break time. That helps us and everyone respects them for that.

> There used to be culture before, where people were a bit frightened of SMT. But I think that the school has gone through a number of historical changes since I got here. I think now teachers have a good healthy respect for SMT. (Karl)

Isla also felt that the power dynamics in the academy were a positive influence; she was in the process of transitioning from a lead teacher role to a role within the senior management team. She illustrated a form tutor system, whereby teachers and staff who operate at different levels within the school are linked together to lead a form group. Working with staff at the different levels was perceived as a mechanism for addressing any power imbalances within the school.

> In terms of SMT, I would say it was quite an equal relationship. I think a class teacher might think differently though. Initially, my role here was as a lead teacher, and I thought SMT were more powerful than me. Now that I have moved into SMT, I recognise how very supportive they are. I have found SMT and college managers to be approachable, and this diminishes any kind of imbalance. SMT are held in high regard here, but they have a certain amount of power over other staff.

> Our form tutor (FT) system means that every single member of staff is a form tutor, and that means an SMT member could work closely with a class teacher and share the responsibility for students in a form group. I think this reduces power relationships within the

school too, because everyone is working together, every single day. So, you might have someone quite senior working with an office member of staff for example. I think getting to know them at that level reduces any kinds of power relationships. (Isla)

Peter describes a situation whereby he didn't agree with a decision made by an SMT member about collecting student data. However, even though he strongly disagreed, he was instructed to carry it through. He was not able to have his say or give his views on the matter.

I think if you are a leader, you have to be seen to be changing things. You have to be seen to have a solution to a problem and a plan. Regardless of whether that plan is good or bad, it has to be followed through to save face. So this is how a typical scenario goes; here is the problem, here is the solution, everybody thinks it's a rotten idea, but we have to go ahead with it. That sort of thing happens a lot. (Peter)

Max identified definite power relationships within the school; he claimed it was 'typical politics!' He also experienced negative vibes about SMT alliances.

Some staff just look after each other. There are some very personal relationships amongst staff and they just 'click together'. There are definite power relationships with people. Our SMT have definite close relationships, they go out with each other, and often go on holiday with each other. These relationships and this bond they have influences their way of doing things in school. Really, that is a power thing, because they are ascertaining their decision-making through their power of knowing each other outside of work. You have to be careful what you say! You hear comments such as 'Oh well, you know what it's like' and 'Well, you know they go on holiday together don't you. You know they are good friends, be careful what you say'. (Max)

Isla felt that through developing positive relationships with staff, it enabled her to use her own personal power to achieve a goal.

> I think for me, the strongest element of personal power is where I have managed to get a staff member to be on board with an initiative. I have also used my personal power to deal with a staff member in conflict. The way I dealt with it is an example of using my own personal power. (Isla)

All the teachers interviewed considered the senior management to have direct influence on the power relationships within the schools, and believed that the SMT play a crucial role in the way they support or nurture teacher empowerment. Overwhelmingly, the majority of the participants felt that the head teacher and the SMT held the greatest power in the school. In some schools this had a positive effect. The SMT had a strong presence around the school, and they were out on the corridors and were on hand to support teachers with everyday issues and challenging students. This was particularly noted by teachers who worked in academies. In some schools, power was used in a negative way, when SMT forced through decisions without consultation and were seen to have favourites. Some staff were also not held to account in the same way as others.

Relationships: In With the In-crowd

All teachers come with their individual sets of beliefs, values and perspectives, all of which influence how they relate and communicate with people across the school organisation. Developing positive relationships between teachers and senior management can often be challenging, particularly when schools are experiencing periods of change. Diane felt that she had a positive relationship with SMT at her school. She felt that she could approach them directly, and did so, when she disagreed with the new cutlery system being introduced in the canteen. Her strong personal beliefs about the environment drove her to instigate change.

> I personally think that if something is generally wrong, I will go and do something about it. I think that it is just me and the way I am.

I strongly want to preserve the environment and when the school changed to plastic cutlery, I went mental! I went straight to the head teacher and said, 'What are we doing? This is not right!' and I gave all the reasons! As a result there is no plastic cutlery anymore, it got changed back to metal. For me it was both morally and ethically wrong. (Diane)

Diane perceived her relationship with the SMT as positive, and she felt appreciated, and listened to. 'I go in and talk to them like they are human beings' she says; they have an open door policy. She also gained further support from relationships with other teachers whom she met early morning before school started.

There are a few staff that get to school quite early in a morning, and we sit in the staff room and work. We all get on and are supportive of each other, it's a bit of a social gathering, I suppose. These people support me, they know what I'm doing and we get on very well. (Diane)

Lucy describes different groups and associations within her school. She felt that some individuals worked on developing positive relationships with others. This, then influenced how they acted and negotiated others to their point of view. There were others, however, who perhaps didn't pay attention to these relationships and end up frustrated and ostracized by SMT.

I think you have got different groups. Some people are quite outspoken and don't really care what they say; they can be quite opinionated and passionate, and they won't back down. Then, there are those who will think before they speak; they will think carefully before they say things. They will also pick and choose their battles. I feel that I am in that group. You also have people who are like 'Yes sir'; they won't disagree with anything, they will just follow and do what is asked of them, but they might moan about it. I do think you have to be careful, because if you opinionate yourself too much, it's a problem, but if you keep saying yes to things, it is also a problem. Sometimes you need to say no! (Lucy)

Harry talks about how staff view the relationships with the SMT at his school.

> Staff don't like the style of relationships that they have with SMT and they get so frustrated that they do not have a say. Staff have no voice and are fearful. If a member of staff says something negative, SMT respond and its 'See you later, loser'. This is sad, because they are losing really good members of staff. (Harry)

Harry goes on to define the culture created by SMT whereby staff feel that they cannot say anything negative, for fear of some form of retaliation. He says that staff feel they are either 'in or out' with SMT.

> It's just depends who you are and whether you are **'in or out'**. Even though I feel that I am 'in' with SMT, it still affects me to know that some teachers are seen as 'out'. I have line managed someone who is not in favor or 'out' with SMT, and that is really hard! There is a really negative vibe, which makes it so difficult to do your job. It makes me feel so sad. There are some people who are put on support plans that shouldn't be on them. (Harry)

Teachers found it difficult to adjust to new senior management teams, particularly when relationships with the previous SMT had been extremely positive. There was also a shift towards a results driven culture, which focused less on building positive staff relationships.

> When I first started at the school, my relationship with SMT was really positive. I am not saying that I don't get on with SMT now; it's a new team and they are very helpful. However, I think the new SMT want to change as much as they can to show impact, and

everything is scrutinized! I know that things have to be quality as-sured, but there is so much emphasis on data, so much emphasis on people doing the right thing. I think SMT have lost their way a bit! It is a 'them and us' situation. Which means, you can talk to them, but they don't want to listen. It's all very one-sided. I think they have forgotten what it is like to be a teacher. (Harry)

Some of the teacher leaders described positive relationships with SMT. SMT were supportive and approachable and teacher leaders felt that they were able to voice their opinions without fear of refute. Some teacher leaders had a real understanding as to how the school politics worked and chose to 'pick their battles'. They maximized their influence by voicing their opinions at the most appropriate times. Others, on the other hand, felt genuine fear and were unable to speak their truths. To do this could risk being 'in with the out crowd', and be detrimental to their job. How SMT perceived, valued and managed relationships with all staff across the school was key as to whether relationships were positive or negative in nature.

Culture: You Get Out What You Put In

A study conducted by Kabler (2013) in the United States identified the relationship between school culture and teacher leadership. Furthermore, research carried out by Katzenmeyer and Moller (2009) emphasised the need for schools to cultivate a culture which is sympathetic for teacher leadership development. Hence, leadership behaviours operate within cultural settings which incorporate a school culture and ethos. This culture determines not so much what people do, but how they do it. Furthermore, the school's culture shapes how people treat one another, what they expect for their own and others behaviours and belief structures, which underline school practices. A study of teacher leadership in England identified a number of factors which enhanced the development of teacher leadership notably, (supportive culture; supportive structures; strong (SMT) leadership; recognition—and reward; commitment to action enquiry and data richness; high levels of teacher participation and involvement; shared professional practice) all of which were deeply entrenched and apparent in the findings (Muijs & Harris, 2006, p. 267).

Peter experienced supportive structures, having moved from one academy to another, within the same multi academy trust. His experience of the transition had been positive. He describes a positive culture at the academy, which enables him to get on with the job of teaching.

> It's very corporate, which I like. There is a lot of branding, but for me it's the systems here that are very strong. The senior leadership here back-up and enforce the systems. A consistent approach is adopted throughout the school. An example is the behaviour policy in this school; I haven't seen it enforced in other schools, as it is done here. I worked at another school for this Multi Academy Trust (MAT) and then moved here. I had no problems dropping in here as the systems are the same. I knew what the expectations were, knew what the procedures were and sanctions, etc. Having really strong policies really helps me. It's not just the behaviour policy, it's also things such as the marking policy. You know what is expected of you, what you have to do, and more importantly, what you don't need to do. (Peter)

Peter also highlighted how favourable cultural conditions for teacher leadership had been put in place, such as, opportunities for staff to take on different roles.

> If you want to have impact at a particular level in the school, there are roles available which teachers can sign up for. For example, a recently qualified teacher was interested in going on to do some form of pastoral role, looking at behaviour data and innovative strategies. He was encouraged to take on this role, even though he had not been at the school long. This role allowed him the opportunity to feedback findings from research and give recommendations directly to the head teacher. There are a whole variety of roles you can go for. You have to apply for the roles and I suspect that if you have a certain skill, they may encourage you to apply for a specific role. You do get payment for the role, a low Teaching and Learning

Reward (TLR). So, if you feel that you want to implement change in the school, there are roles that you can apply for and get involved in. (Peter)

In this case, the academy is providing opportunities for internal promotions and professional development across different disciplines in the school. There appears to be clear hierarchies which facilitate teacher leadership and cultivate positive school culture; this then supports teacher leadership. Muijs and Harris (2006) emphasise the need for optimum cultural and structural conditions to exist for teacher leadership to flourish. Giving leadership responsibility helps to generate the internal conditions for change.

Schools represent a community and individuals can be involved in a complex network of relationships within the school and the school community. What is more, the way in which individuals are treated and how they relate to each other within the organisation affects their attitude towards the institution (Danielson, 2006). Lucy was impressed with the SMT at her school and their efforts to praise teachers through spotlighting individuals at whole school meetings and handing out little notes of thanks.

At briefing, SMT put teachers' names up; we call it 'spotlighting'. SMT say, 'We saw this this week; this was really good'. This is really nice, and a little boost on a Monday morning. SMT have also started writing little postcards to say thank you. SMT also write something positive that they saw in your lesson and leave it on your desk. It's a nice little pick me up when you receive one. I think generally, British people don't praise each other enough. We don't seem to put value on giving each other a pat on the back; we are supportive, but I don't think we go about praising one another enough. I think there is a need for that in teaching. If you consider the impact that praise has on a student, well, it's the same for teachers. It gives you a buzz. (Lucy)

In both of the situations above, the SMT is seeking to develop a culture of clear expectations, consistency and healthy respect for each other. The research on teacher leadership concludes that the headteacher's support is essential to the success of shared or distributed leadership (Muijs & Harris, 2003). The SMT should not only actively encourage teachers to take on leadership roles and engage in professional development, they should also coordinate a shared vision. After a change in leadership, Diane felt that she wanted to clarify the future direction for her particular subject area. The head teacher welcomed her discussion regarding the vision for the faculty and how this fit with the wider school:

> Anything that you want to do at this school is supported within reason. I had a meeting yesterday about the vision for my department. The leadership for this area has changed and so I wanted to know that we were still on the same path. I wanted to know whether the new leadership had a different agenda. I always met regularly with the previous head, we had a shared vision and I knew what the expectations were. I wanted to make sure that the new leadership were still going in the same direction. The meeting was really positive. (Diane)

> If you want to go on a course or a workshop, SMT will find a way to support you. They will find the money from somewhere, particularly if they think it is going to have a positive impact. I think impact is important; everything you do has to have an impact on something within the community or on a particular group of students. (Diane)

In contrast, Jo describes the culture in his school as one which is highly focused on accountability and teacher surveillance. Although he didn't experience this situation personally, he witnessed it happening to a work colleague. Not only did Jo feel powerless to do anything about the situation, it affected his own attitude and perception of the senior management of the school. He said that he felt sad to be a part of it.

> Teachers have no say! I think some staff challenge things, but whether it's listened to or not is something else. It is very sad that I am

currently in a school whereby, if you say something that SMT don't like, then you are 'eyeballed' or investigated. SMT will try and put you on a support plan; it's really not a nice environment to work in. Luckily, for me, I am not in that position at all. I did though, have the unfortunate experience of having to put a teacher on a support plan. I was basically told by SMT to put him on a support plan. I discussed the matter with SMT and questioned them as to whether we had done enough to support this teacher before placing him on the support plan. I also questioned them as to whether they had actually got enough evidence to put this person on a support plan. The answer from SMT was 'actually, no we don't'. I was still made to do it. I felt that that I was not in a position of power to refuse. That teacher is now really demoralised and demotivated about everything. The process had a negative impact on that member of staff and on me. (Jo)

As was in Jo's case, merely witnessing unethical practices or happenings to work colleagues affected his sense of power. Even though he was not directly affected by decisions or events, he felt powerless to support a colleague. It mattered to him and affected his view of the culture of the school. The overall culture undermined his ability to work collaboratively with his colleague; it was a case of 'put him on a support plan, do as we say'. SMT were not prepared to listen to Jo's more supportive efforts to work with his colleague. Accountability, will always be high on the agenda in our schools. When this is coupled with support, mutual respect and recognition, the overarching school culture is optimistic and progressive. But when this is driven by mistrust, heavy surveillance and without care, the culture can be toxic and staff can feel undervalued and demoralised. This study revealed contrasting cultures in academies and state maintained schools. The academy culture appeared more progressive, with the SMT implementing supportive structures and providing new opportunities for teacher leaders. Here they were recognising and rewarding professional practice as suggested by Muijs and Harris, (2006, p. 967). In the maintained schools, this was not the case. The teacher leaders interviewed talked about their fear of speaking out, fear of saying something that the SMT may not agree with, and that could lead to negative consequences. An important point to make here though, is that we must not draw conclusions that the culture in all academies is positive, and in all maintained schools the culture is negative; this is definitely not the case. The residing culture in both types of school can often be reflective of the OFSTED grading, that a school is currently operating under. Furthermore, the stage that the school is at, in their journey towards improvement. What we can derive from this is that schools benefit most from teacher leaders' work when there is trust, open communication, supportive structures and planned time to work collaboratively with colleagues.

Value Teacher Expertise

Danielson (2006) maintains that whilst schools recognise the value of teacher expertise, it is very rarely acted upon or tapped into for planning and improvement. This pertains to the fact that, if schools are actually interested in improving outcomes for students, that expertise within the school walls must not be ignored. There are many reasons why schools should adopt a culture of professional enquiry, and arguably ongoing learning should be at the centre of this. Though many school systems and structures often reinforce a culture of independency and autonomy, most of the time, teachers don't have time to collaborate with colleagues and engage with meaningful inquiry. Teachers must make considerable effort and inclination to engage and learn from other colleagues. Danielson also maintains that a culture of professional enquiry must be established by the senior colleagues in a school; this again must be a safe and encouraging setting, which enables teachers to take risks. All the teacher leaders interviewed demonstrated a commitment to professional inquiry, and their ideas for change and improvement were clearly situated in a vision of high level learning and hard work by students. Expertise which had impact undoubtedly seemed more evident in schools with specific structures and cultures, and ones which allowed a route for this expertise to thrive. This typifies Isla's experience. She works at a high achieving academy which is currently graded 'Outstanding' by OFSTED.

> The school culture is generally, I believe, one where the students feel like they are here to be pushed. It's a very hard-working day for students, but we foster a culture in which students feel included

and supported. The culture here, is one where teachers sing from the same hymn sheet; it's all about consistency and routines. Teachers are expected to operate at a high level and be at the top of their game. A lot is demanded of teachers here. (Isla)

Karl considered that teacher expertise was utilized well through the professional development sessions held each week at the school. It was an expectation that all staff attend these sessions; they are not voluntary. This would suggest that the SMT encouraged a culture of professional enquiry and provided opportunities for teacher collaboration. Karl also mentioned that the SMT had recently changed the structure and focus of the Continuing Professional Development (CPD) session from CPD sessions where the focus of the training was decided usually by SMT and presented to every teacher, to CPD where teachers chose which session they wanted to go to, dependent on their developmental needs and/or areas of interest. So, it was more like a pick and mix CPD, more bespoke, which appears to make a lot more sense.

All teachers stay for an hour after school on a Monday for CPD to look at new teaching techniques and to share how they have been used in a classroom setting. At this school, we don't feel compartmentalised in terms of teaching and learning. New ideas come from lead teachers who have carried out research or attended training courses. New staff are developed and nurtured. Everyone seems to do that little bit extra here. We have a research team who feedback to us their findings. It is not just about developing their teaching, it is for all teachers and used to benefit students and the school as a whole. (Karl)

Many of the teachers interviewed considered knowledge of their subject to be the main area of what they considered to be their teacher expertise. They also felt that it was critical to remain current and up to date for the benefit of students. Some schools have recognised this by providing time and opportunities for teachers in departments to plan together, to go on courses and to share ideas. Lucy discussed new opportunities for staff to get involved in whole school research projects.

We can get involved in projects that might not necessarily be to do with your role; it might be on something like impact. The lead teachers can go to seminars and we can get guest speakers in. Here we see teacher's roles as multifaceted: there is the teacher role, the teaching and learning aspect, your subject area/knowledge and pastoral. (Lucy)

This particular academy appears to be taking steps forward to encourage teacher leadership. They initiate opportunities for collaboration, and encourage sharing best practice and meaningful enquiry. In the main, the teacher leaders felt that their expertise was valued and encouraged to thrive at a departmental level, but very little was tapped into or used at a whole school level. This may be down to ignorance, but in most cases, the SMT have just not put in the necessary structures.

At a departmental level, I think expertise is used well. But from a whole school perspective, it is not. SMT do recognise good teaching and learning, and they have asked me to share things at a 15-minute forum. The problem is, is that teachers are expected to come in 15 minutes before school, so it's a choice for teachers; it is not really whole school CPD. This school is good at identifying where the teacher expertise is in the school. SMT know where the good pockets of teaching and learning are; however, being able to share that with others in the school is something that I don't think they have got right yet. (Harry)

As a Math's specialist, Harry considered that his knowledge could put to good use to support whole school student data and analysis, but unfortunately, this expertise was not utilised.

Why waste a good resource in a school? I mean, we go to staff meetings about raising the achievements of students. I turn up at those meetings with my data and analysis and the member of SMT, who supposedly is in charge of data, does not appear to understand the principles behind the schools' pathway targets. That is so frustrating. They don't ask me; they don't want any help. This may sound a bit strange, but I think it can be a perceived power thing. The member of SMT does not want to been seen to get help from someone who is a lower rank than them. That's how I look at it; it is very much a 'them and us' kind of thing. (Harry)

Harry's experience really encapsulates just how the relationship between power, culture and structure are intertwined. What has emerged in this particular study is that interplay within school organisations is a key determinant as to whether teacher leadership is effective enough to bring about positive school improvements. This aligns with Acker-Hocevar and Touchton (1999), who state that 'the distribution of power within an institution, is as much a part or a reflection, of its culture as it is of its structures. Structure, culture, and power interpenetrate each other' (p. 21).

This study highlighted the requirements of synergy between structure, culture and power in a school environment. These elements need to work together and complement each other for teacher leadership to develop and to have impact on whole school decision-making and school improvement. If one of these elements is not positive, this can have a knock on effect on the others. External pressures from government and OFSTED greatly influence how our schools operate, how power is distributed and the residing culture in the school. This research highlighted that the leadership style adopted by SMT is very much dependent on where the school is on their school improvement journey. This variable also determines whether or not teacher leaders are utilised effectively for school improvement.

The concept of teacher leadership appeared underdeveloped in the majority of schools that took part in this study. When teacher leaders were asked whether they thought they were a teacher leader, they only associated the concept to formalised roles. The narratives revealed that the participants linked teacher leadership to roles such as curriculum leader or leader of teaching and learning. Very few associated teacher leadership with coaching and mentoring, sharing expertise or collaborative working. So the teacher leaders in this study were more inclined to think of themselves as teacher if their role was formalised, along with an official title. Much of the teacher leaders' work appeared unrecognised, or invisible, not just by the SMT in the school, but also from the teacher leaders themselves. So, how can we make teacher leadership part of the discussion in schools? How do we place it on the agenda as a force to be reckoned with? Furthermore, how do we advance the concept and gain recognition by all, that teacher leadership is a key driver for school improvement?

References

Acker-Hocevar, & M., Touchton, D., (1999). *A model of power as social relationships: Teacher leaders describe the phenomena of effective agency in practice.* Paper presented at American Educational Research Association. Montreal, Quebec, Canada. Retrieved from https://eric.ed.gov/?id=ED456108

Anderson, E. (2011). Leadership reflection: Leading myself to lead others. *The International Journal of Leadership in Public Services, 7*(2), 186–188.

Bacharach, S. (1983). Notes on a political theory of educational organizations. In A. Westoby (Ed.), *Culture and power in educational organizations* (pp. 277–288). Milton Keynes, England: Open University Press. Retrieved from https://files.eric.ed.gov/fulltext/ED243175.pdf

BERA (2018) *Revised ethical guidelines for educational research.* British Educational Research Association. Retrieved from http://www.bera.ac.England/files/guidelines/ethica1.pdf

Blase, J., & Anderson, G.L. (1995). *The micropolitics of educational leadership: From control to empowerment.* London: Cassell.

Brosky, D. (2011). Micropolitics in the school: Teacher leaders' use of political. *The International Journal of Educational Leadership Preparation, 6*(1), 1–11. Retrieved from https://files.eric.ed.gov/fulltext/EJ972880.pdf.

Clarke, K.A. (2013). Factors and conditions impacting teacher leader influence. *Procedia—Social and Behavioural Science, 106*(1), 1222–1231. Retrieved from https://www.sciencedirect.com/science/article/pii/S1877042813047605

Danielson, C. (2006). *Teacher leadership that strengthens professional practice.* Alexandria, VA: Association for Supervision & Curriculum Development. Retrieved from http://ebookcentral.proquest.com/lib/hud/detail.action?docID=3002154

Glesne, C. (Ed.) (2011). *Becoming qualitative researchers: An introduction* (4th ed.). London: Pearson.

Hargreaves, A., & Fullan, M. (1998). *What's worth fighting for out there?* New York: Teachers College Press.

Helm, C. (1989). Cultural and symbolic leadership in Catholic elementary schools: An ethnographic study (Unpublished doctoral dissertation). Catholic University of America, Washington, DC.

Kabler, A.L. (2013). *Understanding the relationship between school culture and teacher leadership.* Phoenix, Arizona: Grand Canyon University.

Katzenmeyer, M., & Moller, G. (2009). *Helping teachers develop as leaders.* Thousand Oaks, California: Corwin.

Lambert, L. (2003a). *Leadership capacity for lasting school improvement.* Alexandria, VA: The Association for Supervision and Curriculum Development.

Lambert, L. (2003b) Leadership redefined: an evocative context for teacher leadership, *School Leadership & Management, 23*(4), 421–430. https://doi.org/10.1080/ 1363243032000150953

Leithwood, K., Jantzi, D., & Steinbach, R. (1999). *Changing leadership for changing times.* Philadelphia, PA: Open University Press.

Muijs, D., & Harris, A. (2003). Teacher leadership: Improvement through empowerment? An overview of the literature. *Educational Management Administration & Leadership, 31*(4), 437–48.

Muijs, D., & Harris, A. (2006). Teacher led school improvement: Teacher leadership in the UK. *Teaching and Teacher Education, 22*(8), 961–972. https://doi.org/ 10.1016/j.tate.2006.04.010

Pellicer, L.O., Anderson, L.W., Keefe, J.W., Kelley, E.A., & McCleary, L. (1990). High school leaders and their schools:. Profiles of effectiveness. Reston, VA: *National Association of Secondary School Principals.* Retrieved from https:// files.eric.ed.gov/fulltext/ED319139.pdf

Rosenholz, S. (1989). *Teachers' workplace: The social organisation of schools.* New York: Teachers College Press.

Sickler, J.L. (1988). Teachers in charge: Empowering the professionals. *Phi Delta Kappan, 69*(6) 354–375. Retrieved from https://eric.ed.gov/?id=EJ364792

Sisken, L.S., & Little, J.W. (1995). *The subject in question: Departmental organization and the high school.* New York, NY: Teachers College Press.

Wasley, P.A. (1991). *Teachers who lead: The rhetoric of reform and the realities of practice.* New York: Teachers College Press.

Weiss, C., & Cambone, J. (2000). *Principals, shared decision making and school reform.* In *The Jossey-Bass reader on educational leadership* (pp. 366–389). Chicago: Jossey-Bass.

Weston, D. (2018). *Five solutions for teacher retention and development.* Retrieved from https://schoolsweek.co.England/five-solutions-for-teacher-retention-and-development/

CHAPTER THREE

Reflection

Susan Timmins

THERE IS SOMETHING PRETTY special about teacher leaders! In the right context, teacher leaders position themselves to 'do good' in a school. They demonstrate an innate sense of going 'above and beyond' and do their absolute best for the students that they teach. They care about students beyond the classroom, taking a holistic approach, rather than seeing students as a set of outcomes or results. Teacher leaders in this study displayed a prominent 'moral identity' in their concept of themselves (Oplatka, 2016, p. 11), an affiliation with ideals of 'moral leadership' such as those raised by Sergionvanni (1999) and Foster (1986) and a sense that they are 'leaders for social justice' (Brooks, 2009, cited in Normore, 2010, p. 217). These teacher leaders were guided by ethical and moral values that influenced their actions towards inequality and provided second chances for students in their schools.

Developing meaningful relationships with staff and students was extremely important to all the teacher leaders interviewed in this study. Some referred to their school as a community and demonstrated a commitment to developing relationships with other people and other schools, colleges and higher education institutions within and outside their own multi-academy trust (MAT). There was a sense of them being 'bridge builders', individuals who unite people, ideas and resources to advance equity issues in their school (Merchant and Shoho, 2010). Developing positive relationships with other staff and the senior managers was perceived as a platform for teacher leaders to exercise agency and influence the decision-making. A number of the teachers, again particularly in the academies, thought relationships with the SMT were very positive; all were approachable and offered support. Senior leaders were praised for their 'strong presence' in and around school; many perceived this as a great support. Feeling valued and listened to by the SMT meant that the teachers could feedback honestly without fear of being ostracised. What was plain to see was the vision of the SMT and how they valued and managed these relationships. This was a key determinant as to whether relationships generally across the school were of a positive or negative nature and how teacher empowerment was cultivated

However, as I alluded to in the earlier chapter, for teacher leaders to flourish in their role, the right context is required. As found in this research, many barriers continue to exist in schools and the teacher leader role continues to appear insignificant to many government bodies and senior managers who lead schools in England today. For example, OFSTED poses great influence on leadership styles and how power and decision-making is distributed across the school and afforded to teacher leaders. For the schools in which the teacher leaders in this study worked, the OFSTED grade awarded appeared to be a crucial determinant of the residing school culture. Hallinger notes 'the stage a school is at in the improvement cycle and how it sees itself are important factors in establishing its internal culture' (as cited in Miller, 2018, p. 134). Teachers at all levels within a school, in an OFSTED category of grade 3 or below, are under immense pressure to improve. In these instances, senior managers seem to adopt a 'top down' management style where they make all the decisions and teachers just have to conform and get on with it. The SMT can often be perceived as if they are there to 'sort teachers out', to rid the school of ineffectiveness. This in turn can create division between 'old staff and new staff'. Within this study, this manifested itself in some cases with individualist decision-making, with some senior leaders wanting to demonstrate impact quickly, massaging their own ego, not necessarily for the good of students or staff. Oplatka (2016) refers to this approach as 'irresponsible leadership' (IRL) and the 'dark side of leadership'. Not surprisingly, the effects of IRL are not positive and often results in non-retention of teachers, poor student well-being and an 'unethical school climate, lack of social responsibility in the teacher lounge, and school failure' (Oplatka, 2016, p. 1). Disappointingly, some teacher leaders passively accept this dominant and autocratic style of leadership, claiming to accept decisions made by the SMT as they are the ones in a position of power. One respondent claimed, 'Whatever decisions they make, whether you agree with it or not, you just do it!' (Karl). Some also pointed out that it was the SMT's job to make the decisions, since they hold a certain position in the school and this gives them the right to do so. Furthermore, they pointed out that the SMT were paid a lot of money to lead a school. The reality is that these teacher leaders are paralysed into thinking that they cannot or should not disturb the status quo by questioning decisions made further up the chain.

Furthermore, in this study there appeared to be a distinct polarisation between leadership approaches adopted in state-maintained schools as opposed to academies. For example, some of the teacher leaders in academies referred to their context as very businesslike, a commercial enterprise with a strong focus on student achievement. Critics of academies would argue that this type of leadership is less concerned with the common good, and more about the view that students are clients and the school functions in some form of competitive educational market that focuses less on the aim of educating children. In comparison, the state-maintained schools in this study, whilst still having a huge emphasis on accountability and results, appeared less corporate and more about maintaining the unique characteristics of the school. Consequently, the leadership style adopted in these schools appeared more in tune or more influenced by 'internal and personal factors' (Miller, 2018, p. 121). Miller asserts that each school has its own specific context and that the practice of leadership cannot be a 'one size fits all'. Furthermore, 'school leaders cannot simply transfer what worked in one school into another one, no matter how well they have worked elsewhere or in the past'. (Miller, 2018, p. 121).

The teacher leader role provides an opportunity for purposeful collaboration, the opportunity to influence others and the opportunity to transform pedagogy. Once the academies in this study had become established or achieved a 'Good' or 'Outstanding' OFSTED rating, they assumed a more consultative and collaborative approach. They became interested in staff voice, developed roles and created a culture where teacher leaders can develop. The study also revealed that some academies seemed to be making attempts to create structures to enable teacher leadership to flourish. In two academies, there were a number of direct efforts to create favourable cultural conditions to develop teacher leadership, such as lead teacher roles, focusing on pastoral, research or other innovative whole school improvement initiatives. In addition, they provided time for teachers to collaborate, plan together, and share practice and learn from each other. Importantly, they created a culture of professional enquiry, and this was down to the senior management team buying in and driving this type of professional school culture.

In most schools, however, teacher leaders considered that there was a general ceiling to their decision-making; they were involved and felt enabled to make decisions at a departmental level, but not whole school. Teacher leaders were also quick to identify when senior management put in place a form of contrived collegiality or offered 'token gestures' in the decision-making process. Where staff are consulted just for show, they are not really listened to, their feedback is ignored and decisions are made regardless. Even those in more formal teacher leader roles such as a curriculum leader felt that sometimes the decision-making was a two-way process, but other times, it was literally, this is what is happening, and it was up to curriculum leaders to ensure that the new process or initiative was implemented in the department. No opportunities, therefore, were given for discussion, responses and feedback. Teachers felt that the decision-making was something that was 'done at them' rather than with them. This also presented teacher leaders with some difficult conversations to have with colleagues, when trying to implement a decision for which they themselves had often made no contribution.

In the main, teacher leaders believed that deep knowledge and staying current in the area of subject specialism was considered to be their expertise. This knowledge of their subject afforded them the power to make decisions within their own department. Once again, it was the academies that were utilising this valuable source to support effective whole school improvement, as they provided lead teachers with opportunities to share research and new pedagogical practice. At one academy, the SMT at staff meetings regularly highlighted good practice that they had observed during learning walks and they encouraged teachers to share their practices with others. In this academy, changes were made to professional development from a 'one size fits all' approach to a 'pick and mix' style whereby staff chose which CPD session to attend, based on their individual developmental needs. Unfortunately, this was not the case at some schools and resulted in some teachers feeling very frustrated and questioning senior managers who appeared to make decisions which were more about demonstrating impact to further their own careers than concentrating on what is best for the students. This was seen to be intensified in those schools highly fixated on accountability, or if a school had been graded 'Requires Improvement' or 'Inadequate' by OFSTED.

The role of the head teacher in developing teacher leadership is paramount. Success was gained when they promoted well-defined communication channels, implemented supportive structures and provided professional development opportunities to share in leadership tasks. Prior to engaging in this research, the term 'teacher leadership' was a new concept for me even though I have worked in secondary schools in England for more than 15 years. My understanding of teacher leadership was strictly confined to those teachers who took on more formal roles such as that of assistant head teacher, deputy head teacher or head teacher/principal. I now recognise myself as a teacher leader having worked in schools in the North of England, all of which were in communities experiencing high deprivation, social issues and poverty. The school community and the teachers were the only constant in many of the children's lives, and I never underestimated the power I held as a teacher to influence change for the children I taught. Whilst taking on various formal leadership roles, I too observed and experienced the many obstacles that teacher leaders continue to face day to day, and having heard the teacher leaders' experiences in this study, have come to the conclusion that the teacher leadership movement is making slow progress.

What has emerged from this study, however, is the apparent synergistic nature of agency, power and school culture and how all aspects appear inter-related and are dependent on each other. A strong positive school culture with enabling structures fosters an environment whereby teacher leaders are empowered to innovate, develop pedagogy and influence the work of others. Although attempts have been made in some academies, such as developing more formal teacher leaders' roles, distributing decision-making and empowering teachers, it is fair to argue that things have not gone far enough.

This study also highlights that teacher leaders are operating in contexts heavily focused on accountability, but where this is coupled with top-down control and surveillance from SMT, it leads to disempowerment, discouragement and passivity. As stated by the National Education Union (2019), the accountability regime needs to be 'reset and rebalanced', allowing teachers to focus on teaching and supporting children and enabling teacher leaders with the SMT to develop learning communities whereby staff unite and share ideas and resources to advance equity in schools (Merchant and Shoho, 2010). Politicians and some senior managers are just not putting teachers first; they perceive teachers' roles as almost robotic, teaching to the test and ticking boxes, rather than seeing teachers as highly qualified and skilled individuals. The notion of teacher leaders is nonexistent in their eyes. The 12 individuals who took part in this research are confirmation that they do exist, albeit their skills are not utilised to the fullest.

So what can be done to ensure that the teacher leader movement makes better progress? In the first instance, we have a lot to do to raise the professional status of teachers in England, and I believe this drive can come from within our schools. Teacher leaders need to come forward and make a stand for how they believe our children should be educated and how our schools should be led into the future. No more passive acceptance of systems and testing which have a damaging impact on children, but marching forward bravely disrupting the status quo for equality, social justice and our future generations. Teacher leaders can hope to gain the backing from the people in power if they are relentless and always lead for the benefit of the children that they teach. Head teachers must identify with the concept of teacher leadership and believe that successful school leadership can be gained from many individuals in the organisation, not just those in formally recognised roles. Utilising this existing resource within their organisations will go some way to gaining higher recognition for existing teachers in the profession.

Many of the teacher leaders who participated in this study were not familiar with the term *teacher leader*, as it is not a term used freely in schools in England. Leadership roles tend to be formal roles such as assistant headteacher, senior leader or middle leader. Whilst some of the participants had roles such as lead teacher, this was formalised, usually in the form of a promotion with additional payment. Teacher training providers could help promote the teacher leadership concept to new recruits to the profession. That said, teachers who strive for higher professional status must also possess an innate willingness to go above and beyond, and not underestimate the hard work and extra effort that this will entail. A greater obstacle, however, could be the senior management's willingness to share their power with others in the organisation. OFSTED could play a significant role in promoting both a shared leadership approach and the concept of teacher leadership by specifically referring to the concept of teacher leadership and distributed leadership in their inspection framework rather than the broad statement of 'shared values, policies and practice' (OFSTED, 2019, p. 11). From experience we know that when OFSTED makes it a focus area, school leaders will respond and implement any changes necessary to gain a good evaluation during inspection.

References

Foster, W (1986). *Paradigms and promises: New approaches to educational administration*. Buffalo, NY: Promethean Books.

Merchant, B.M. and Shoho, A.R. (2010). Bridge people: civic and educational leaders for social justice. In C. Marshall, C. and M. Oliva (Eds.), *Leadership for social justice* (2nd ed., pp. 120–138). Boston, MA.: Allyn & Bacon.

Miller, P.W. (2018). *The nature of school leadership: Global practice perspectives*. Retrieved from http://ebookcentral.proquest.com

National Education Union. (2019). *The state of education: Workload*. Retrieved from https://neu.org.uk/press-releases/state-education-workload

Normore, A.H. (Ed.). (2010). *Global perspective on educational leadership reform: The development and preparation of leaders of learning and learners of leadership*. United Kingdom: Emerald Group Publishing Ltd.

OFSTED (2019). *The education inspection framework*. (190015). Retrieved from https://assets.publishing.service.gov.uk/governmentuploads/system/uploads/attachment_ datafile/801429/Education_inspection_framewrok.pdf

Oplatka, I. (2016). Irresponsible leadership" and unethical practices in schools: A conceptual framework of the "dark side" of educational leadership." In *The dark side of leadership: Identifying and overcoming unethical practice in organizations*, 1–18. Retrieved from: https://doi.org/10.1108/S1479-36602016000026001

Sergionvanni, T. J (1999). *Rethinking leadership: A collection of articles*. Arlington Heights, IL: Skylight Training and Publishing.

Teacher Leadership in Jamaica

CHAPTER FOUR

Critical Perspectives on Teacher Leadership in Jamaica

CARMEL ROOFE

T HE USE OF THE term *teacher leadership* has existed in countries such as the United States, Canada and Australia for more than half a century (Lee-Piggott, 2014). However, the concept is fairly new within the Jamaican context and is now only being given much attention. In fact, a colleague who designs courses at a teacher education institution that has offered programmes in Jamaica for 60 years, lamented the challenges experienced in 2013 when trying to acquire approval for a course titled *teacher leadership*. She said that the challenges arose because many committee members had not heard of such a term and felt that perhaps it should be a topic in a course but not a course in and of itself. Nonetheless, she advocated and had support from other colleagues who were aware of the breadth and depth of the concept. The course was eventually granted approval. Fast forward to 2018 and the course has become a favourite amongst students pursuing graduate degrees at the said university. The course introduces and explores the concept of teacher leadership through providing participants with the skills and dispositions to influence school culture, facilitate excellence in practice, build successful teams and improve student achievement (School of Education, EDTE6024, 2011).

Though the concept of teacher leadership has seemingly evolved in the

Jamaican space through academics in higher education institutions, an understanding of the practice and value of teacher leadership to overall school improvement seems to be missing. Given the National Education Inspectorate (NEI) report of 2016 that there are 'some schools that receive the requisite resources and inputs, but the quality of teaching and school leadership do not provide the value-added that improves students' outcomes' (p. 2), it behooves us to make deliberate attempts and commitments toward the theory and practice of teacher leadership. Furthermore, at the K-12 level, recognition is needed by policymakers, school leaders and teachers of the value of teacher leadership in helping to improve the K-12 education system.

A starting point for our discussion then is to examine the literature available on teacher leadership in the Jamaican context. A search for literature in this context reveals a conference presentation in Trinidad by Davies in 2013, titled, *Teacher leadership: Are Jamaican schools ready to embrace the concept?* and a book chapter publication in the same year by McCallum titled, *Teachers as leaders: building the middle leadership base in Jamaican schools*. Both researchers are from the same institution and took a different perspective on teacher leadership. The conference presentation by Davies explored the question: Are Jamaican schools ready to embrace the concept of teacher leadership? In her study, though recognising that there is a definition problem of the concept 'teacher leadership', she aligns her definition of teacher leadership with that generally offered by scholars in the field (Angelle & DeHart, 2016; York-Barr & Duke, 2004). Davies (2013) defined a teacher leader as a specially motivated individual who is driven by an almost moral imperative to commit to and work for the betterment of students, colleagues and the entire school. The findings shared from her research suggest that teachers and principals had mixed reactions to the concept of teachers as leaders, including some principals not supportive of teacher leaders due to the lack of understanding of the concept and some teachers who felt that it is really more work for them. She concluded that as more students pursue the teacher leadership course in their Masters programme, teachers and principals may become more aware of the benefits of teacher leadership, thereby valuing its importance in school transformation.

McCallum (2013) examined the issue of teacher leadership as an opportunity for building the middle leadership base in Jamaican schools. In her study, middle leadership constitutes those who are heads of department and grade supervisors in their schools. She offers two justifications for teacher leadership as an opportunity to build middle leadership. These are: (1) Opportunities for teacher leadership abound in the Jamaican context given the plethora of curriculum and school related matters for which teachers are responsible. (2) Only a few opportunities exist for teachers to assume formal leadership roles and many of these are not rotational. In her study, McCallum focused on the role of teacher leaders as mentors. To that end, she defined teacher leaders as 'experienced expert teachers who function in a supportive and nurturing role as they assist novice and beginning teachers to make the transition to practice' (p. 107). McCallum's study is valuable and provides useful insights for teacher preparation. The teacher mentors in her study were asked to indicate whether they regarded themselves as teacher leaders. The finding indicated that a majority (67%) of the participants did not see themselves as teacher leaders, and those who saw themselves as teacher leaders equated their role to that of modeling (p. 120). This led Mc-Callum to conclude that the teacher mentors seemed less clear about teacher leadership being a role they performed as teacher mentors.

The research presented here is necessary and timely for two main reasons: (1) sharing perspectives from the context of a developing country, which adds to the body of literature locally and internationally and (2) providing research-based documentary accounts of what characterises teacher leadership in this context. These accounts will not only illuminate the issue, but can serve as teaching tools for policy makers and practitioners. Furthermore, the research presented here may serve to inspire teachers to become teacher leaders and motivate teacher leaders to continue their quest. Consequently, this study may be the impetus for lasting, sustainable change in Jamaica.

Overview of Schooling in Jamaica

Jamaica is a small island state situated in the Commonwealth Caribbean with a population of approximately 2.8 million. Schooling in the Jamaican context is highly structured and highly valued by all stakeholders. The Ministry of Education, Youth and Information as the central authority, is responsible for the management and administration of schools and carries out the education mandate of the government. Schools are grouped according to six regions across the island. These regional offices unite with the central office to ensure support, monitoring and effective functioning of the education system in Jamaica (Ministry of Education, Youth and Information, 2019).

Schooling is offered at the early childhood (3–5 years old), primary (6–11 years old), secondary (12–17 years old) and post-secondary levels in different types of institutions. Schooling at the early childhood level is provided in community and government operated basic schools, infant schools and infant departments in primary schools and kindergartens of privately-operated schools. These institutions are supervised by the Early Childhood Commission, an arm of the government established in 2005 to ensure standards in this sector.

Schooling at the primary level is offered in three types of schools: public primary, primary departments of primary and junior high schools, and in private (preparatory schools) schools for six years. Primary and preparatory schools offer six years of education while primary and junior high schools offer nine years of education. Students undergo several standardised tests at major transitional points during their school life. The results from these tests are used to screen students for the next level of learning and provide remediation where necessary. Additionally, the results of these tests are used to hold school personnel accountable.

At the secondary level of schooling, there are different types of schools, which also means students with varying ability levels, resources and support. Schools that were built during the British rule are referred to as *traditional high schools*, and schools that were built after independence are referred to as *non-traditional high schools* or *upgraded high schools*. Traditional high schools are considered to have better quality resources and facilities, a traditional grammar type curriculum, more academically gifted students and better parental support. For both traditional and non-traditional high schools, schooling at the secondary level consists of two cycles. The first cycle begins at grades 7–9 of all ages, primary and junior high, high schools and technical and independent or private high schools (Ministry of Education, 2019).

The National Standards Curriculum (NSC) implemented in 2016 guides teaching and learning at grades 1–6 of primary schools and grades 7–9 of secondary schools. It seeks to enhance the quality of education offered to learners and improve the general academic performance, attitude and behaviour of students, which is intended to lead to the positive shaping of the national, social and economic fabric (Ministry of Education, Youth and Information, 2016). The Ministry Paper 47 states that the NSC is intended to improve educational outcomes through inspiring and providing greater opportunities for all learners via an inclusive approach catering to the needs of all students and leading to the positive shaping of the country's social and economic fabric (Ministry of Education, Youth and Information, 2016). Consequently, emphasis is placed on the use of Information and Communication Technologies, project-based learning and problem-solving, with Science, Technology, Engineering and Mathematics or Science, Technology, Engineering, Arts and Mathematics (STEM/STEAM) integrated at all levels (Ministry of Education, Youth and Information, 2017). Since 2018–19, the Primary Exit Profile (PEP) has been implemented, involving a series of assessments that students complete in three categories: performance task, ability test and curriculum-based tests. These tests begin in grade 4 and end in grade 6, and their results are used to place students in secondary schools at the end of grade 6 (Jamaica Information Service, 2018).

The NSC and PEP are expected to allow for greater accountability at the school level and better articulation across grade levels. Both reforms are critical to the skills that policymakers indicate students need to develop to be ready for the global village as 21st-century citizens.

The second cycle of secondary school is offered in grades 10 to 11 of traditional and non-traditional high schools. At the end of grade 11, students may continue to grade 12 or 13, which is optional, depending on their examination results at the end of grade 11 or their career path. Additionally, at the end of secondary education, students may transition to the world of work or pursue further education in technical vocational institutions, community colleges, teachers' colleges or universities. In 2016, the Minister of Education, Youth and Information announced that starting September 2016, an additional two years of high school should be compulsory for all students. However, this has not been fully implemented as not all high schools adhere to this principle. The outcomes of the second cycle of secondary schooling in Jamaica highly dictate what happens to a student after completing secondary education. Therefore, the second cycle of secondary schooling is examination oriented. The results of the examinations are used to judge teachers and schools and help to influence parents' preferred choice of school. As a result, these examinations may influence some teachers' willingness to take on additional roles and responsibilities in school.

Jamaica boasts a record of increased access to education but struggles with the issue of offering quality education (UNICEF, 2011; USAID, 2013). Wide disparities exist amongst schools as it relates to resources, abilities of learners and the social milieu. Increasingly, schooling is fraught with issues of violence amongst students giving rise to an increase in maladaptive behaviour (National Education Inspectorate Report, 2015; Edwards-Kerr, 2013). School leaders therefore need the help of teacher leaders to transform student outcomes. Teacher leaders can play a critical role given that teachers tend to listen to their colleagues, are aware of the day-to-day needs of students, are closer to issues in the surrounding community and interface more intimately with parents and other stakeholders at the school level (Clandinin & Connelly, 1992). In Jamaica there is a heavy emphasis on test scores as accountability resulting in a performativity culture. This often sets up the principal to bear the brunt of the burden for the success of a school. Additionally, the context of schools in Jamaica is based on a colonial heritage, which suggests that one group (headmaster/principal/supervisor) must exercise power over the other and that the autonomy of particular groups must be curtailed and strictly managed. The traditional role of the principal is entrenched in the principal as the sole authority and decision-maker with teachers as subordinates. However, given emphasis on quality education in the era of globalisation, no longer can the principal be the sole authority and classroom teachers seen as subjects and followers without a vocal voice in decision-making. Today's principalship requires distributed leadership where efforts are made to empower teachers to complement their role (Hutton, 2013). I recognise, however, that the concept of teacher leadership in a country struggling to shed the traditional role of the principal as sole leader of a school requires unpacking to examine how teachers in Jamaica are prepared for their roles in this context.

Teacher Preparation in Jamaica

Teachers are prepared for their roles through pre-service and in-service training programmes. Teachers may pursue these programmes through colleges dedicated solely to training teachers or through education departments within universities. During pre-service programmes, student teachers follow the traditional model of pursuing courses in college/university classrooms followed by extended periods of practicum. In these pre-service programmes, student teachers are exposed to foundational education knowledge, content and pedagogical knowledge and supervised field practice (Joint Board of Teacher Education, 2012). Upon completion students are awarded a bachelor's degree.

The in-service teacher preparation route is for those teachers who have entered the teaching profession through employment with a first degree and are not teacher trained, and therefore will pursue a postgraduate diploma in education while teaching. The aim of the postgraduate degree programme is to provide such individuals with exposure to pedagogical skills. Other in-service training programmes include teachers pursuing advanced degrees in masters and doctoral programmes.

It is expected that both pre-service and in-service programmes when undertaken will provide teachers with the skills they need to contribute to quality student outcomes. More specifically, as outlined in Jamaica's Vision 2030, teacher preparation aims to provide 'A quality teacher education system driving human, economic and social development' through preparing 'teaching professionals who are reflective, socially conscious, highly proficient practitioners empowered to develop independent, creative and productive citizens' (p. 133). Many of the reforms in teacher preparation have been linked to Jamaica's national development beginning with emancipation in 1834, to post independence reforms in 1966, 1983, the 1990s and up to the 2000s (George, Wilson, & Plunkett, 2016). These reforms have been aimed at increasing the cadre of teachers and later the quality of teachers to contribute to building the Jamaican society. One of the agencies that emerged from reforms in the 2000s is the Jamaica Teaching Council (JTC). In 2008, as part of the general thrust to reform the education system in Jamaica, the JTC was established with a mandate to professionalise the teaching profession in Jamaica on the basis that teachers are vital to increasing the achievement levels of learners. A remit of the JTC was to establish standards for all educators in Jamaica, including those who train teachers. These standards were to be then used as the basis for greater levels of accountability and professionalism as Jamaica moves toward licensing those who work in the teaching profession. To date, standards have been drafted, but the bill to establish JTC as the governing body for the teaching profession is still being deliberated and has not yet been passed in the House of Parliament. This means that until then, JTC cannot fully carry out its mandate.

A study undertaken by the University of Technology in 2015 to support the work of the Jamaica Tertiary Education Commission as it performs its role in reforming tertiary education highlighted that teachers indicated a lack of field experience in their training and lack of adequate induction to prepare them for the work they need to do in schools (George, Wilson, & Plunkett, 2016). This also aligns with findings from similar studies on beginning teachers carried out by Roofe (2014) and Neil-Johnson and Roofe (2017). Such findings suggest that though reform efforts are ongoing, a much more targeted approach is needed as it relates to capacity building for teachers.

Teacher leadership is underpinned by the philosophy that classroom teachers are critical to the overall improvement of schools and their success. In light of this philosophy, perhaps more attention needs to be given to the work of teacher educators and the skills they possess or need to possess, in order to in turn adequately equip teachers with the skills needed for the 21st century. In Jamaica, those who enter higher education to train teachers are usually experienced former teachers who possess at least a bachelor's degree with most holding a master's degree. However, while there is a growing body of research (Bailey, 2007; Hordatt-Gentles, 2003; Mayne, 2012; Roofe, Bezzina, & Holness, 2017) on teacher educators in Jamaica, more research is needed to understand them and to inform policy directions for implementing the most appropriate mechanism to support them in preparing teachers for the nature of schools and the roles involved.

References

Angelle, P. S. & DeHart, C. A. (2016). Comparison and evaluation of four models of teacher leadership, *Research in Educational Administration & Leadership*, *1*(1), 85–119.

Bailey, E. (2007). Teacher education in a post-colonial context: A phenomenological study of the experience of Jamaican teachers' college lecturers. (Doctoral dissertation, University of Massachusetts). Retrieved from http://scholarworks. umass.edu/dissertations/AAI3254932

Clandinin, D. J., & Connelly, F. M. (1992). Teacher as curriculum maker. In P. Jackson (Ed.), *Handbook of Curriculum Research*, pp. 363–401. New York: MacMillan.

Davies, R. (2013). Teacher leadership: Are Jamaican schools ready to embrace the concept? [PowerPoint Presentation]. School of Education. Biennial Conference

UWI, St. Augustine Campus, Trinidad & Tobago. April 23 – 25, 2013. Retrieved from http://uwispace.sta.uwi.edu/dspace/handle/2139/15778

Edwards-Kerr, D. (2013). A critical perspective on violence in schools. *Caribbean partners for educational progress*. Retrieved from http://www.mona.uwi.edu/cop/groups/eduexchange-questioning-school-violencejamaican-schools-critical-perspective/critical

George, N., Henry-Wilson, M., Plunkett, N. (2016). A case study in Jamaica's reform of teacher education: preparing teachers for the 21st Century Classroom. In C. Hordatt-Gentles (Ed.), *ICET 2016, 60th World Assembly 60th Yearbook of Teacher Education*. Mona, Kingston: UWI School of Education.

Hordatt-Gentles, C. (2003). The pedagogical culture of New College: A critical examination of pedagogy in a Jamaican teachers college (Unpublished doctoral dissertation). OISE, University of Toronto, Canada.

Hutton, D. (2013). High-performing Jamaican principals: Understanding their passion, commitment and abilities. In P. Miller (Ed.), *School leadership in the Caribbean: Perceptions, practices paradigms*. United Kingdom, Symposium Books.

Jamaica Information Service (2018). Get the facts – Primary exit profile (PEP). Retrieved from https://jis.gov.jm/information/get-the-facts/get-the-facts-primary-exit-profile-pep/

Joint Board of Teacher Education, (2012). Aims of teacher training. Retrieved from http://www.jbte.edu.jm/cms/regulations/aims of teacher training.aspx

Lee-Pigott, R. (2014) When teachers lead: An analysis of teacher leadership in one primary school. *Caribbean Curriculum, 22*, 105–132.

Mayne, H. (2012). From roots to blossoms: a description of the shared teaching experiences of Jamaican teacher educators. Retrieved from https://www.ideals.illinois.edu/handle/2142/34262

McCallum, D. (2013). Teachers as leaders: Building the middle leadership base in Jamaican schools. In P. Miller (Ed.), *School leadership in the Caribbean: Perceptions, practices and paradigms*. United Kingdom: Symposium Books.

Ministry of Education, Youth and Information (2016). 2016 Ministry paper 47 the National Standards curriculum (NSC). Retrieved from http://japarliament.gov.jm/index.php/publications/ministry-paper-new/2016-ministry-paper/1678-2016-ministry-papers-47-the-national-standards-cirriculum-nsc

Ministry of Education, Youth and Information (2017). The National Standards Curriculum. Retrieved from https://moey.gov.jm/

Ministry of Education, Youth and Information (2019). The history of the Ministry of Education. Retrieved from https://moey.gov.jm/about

National Education Inspectorate Report. (2016). Chief inspector's report 2016. Retrieved from https://www.nei.org.jm/Portals/0/Content/Documents/C2R1%20Chief%20Inspector's%20Report%202016%20Final.pdf?ver=2018-04-19-115528-887&ver=2018-04-19-115528-887

National Education Inspectorate Report. (2015). Chief inspector's baseline report 2015. Retrieved from http://www.nei.org.jm/Portals/0/Content/ Documents/Chief%20Inspector's %20Baseline%20Report%202015.pdfer=2016-06-23-130247-730

Neil-Johnson, G., & Roofe, C. (2017). Exploring beginning teachers' experiences: Insights for teacher learning and development. *Journal of Education and Development in the Caribbean, 16*(2), 107–130.

Roofe, C. (2014). One size fits all: Perceptions of the revised primary curriculum at grades one to three in Jamaica. *Research in Comparative and International Education, 9*(1), 4–15.

Roofe, C. (2018). Schooling, teachers in Jamaica and social responsibility: Rethinking teacher preparation. *Journal of Social Responsibility, 14*(4), 816–827.

Roofe, C., Bezzina, & Holness, M. (2017). Social justice and the teacher preparation curriculum: A cross cultural analysis. In C. Roofe & C. Bezzina (Eds.), *Intercultural studies in curriculum: Theory, policy and practice* (pp. 17–41). Basingstoke, UK: Palgrave Macmillan.

School of Education, EDTE6024, (2011). Teacher leadership course outline. School of Education, UWI, Mona, department communication.

York-Barr, J., & Duke, K. (2004). What do we know about teacher leadership? Findings from two decades of scholarship. *Review of Educational Research, 74*, 255–316.

UNICEF (2018). Situation analysis of Jamaican children-2018. Retrieved from https://www.unicef.org/jamaica/UNICEF_20180618_SituationAnalysis_web.pdf

USAID. 2013. Midterm performance evaluation of the USAID/Jamaica basic education project: In Support of the Jamaica Education Transformation Project. Accessed 20 July 2015. https://www.mona.uwi.edu/cop/sites/default/files/JETP_Midterm_Performance_Evaluation_Final_Report..pdf

CHAPTER FIVE

The Empirical Study of Teacher Leaders in Jamaica

CARMEL ROOFE

CONSISTENT WITH THE FOCUS of this book, grounded theory and narrative research designs were used to capture the perspectives of teacher leaders working in Jamaican schools. Grounded theory provided an opportunity to contextualise the evidence and ensure its connectivity to the realities of teacher leaders' work in schools within the Jamaican context as I theorised the findings (Creswell, 2012). From this perspective, it can be acknowledged that teacher leaders' work is rooted in the history of schooling in Jamaica, the history of the particular school within which the teachers work, and that responses to the interview questions are not devoid of this history. Using grounded theory was particularly important since there is a dearth of evidence and literature on teacher leadership in the Jamaican context. Narrative design provided the means for understanding the personal day-to-day experiences of teachers as teacher leaders and the meanings they attach to these experiences (Clandinin & Connelly, 1992). The aim therefore was to understand the teacher leaders' experiences within the social context of schools and to provoke thoughts about their work and what they value.

Participants were selected through purposive sampling methods. The researcher contacted two cohorts of graduate students she previously taught in 2016–2018 to solicit their support in identifying participants known to them in their schools who met the following criteria: completed at least a bachelor's degree; currently teaching; demonstrated initiative; collegial; extremely supportive of stakeholders in the school context where he/she worked; actively involved in ongoing professional development and not appointed as senior teacher in their school. The researcher then contacted potential participants to solicit their willingness to participate in the research. Participants were advised of the ethics governing the research process. Twelve teacher leaders located in twelve schools across six parishes in Jamaica expressed willingness and availability to participate in the research. In selecting the participants, the intent was not to provide a representative sample, but to maximise the potential to discover dimensions and conditions surrounding teacher leadership as a construct (Strauss & Corbin, 1998).

Consistent with the protocol agreed on for this collaborative research project across the three countries, and adhering to ethical standards for conducting research, a semi-structured interview protocol consisting of seven questions was used to collect data from each participant. Data collected was recorded and then transcribed. A cyclical, reflexive approach was used in analysing the data from the participants to ensure an emic focus. This entailed using techniques from grounded and narrative research designs as I summarised the data from each participant, identified categories and pattern codes, used memos to conceptualise and theorise, and used constant comparisons to generate themes (Creswell, 2012; Yin, 2011; Strauss & Corbin, 1998). Any anomalies were noted and included as important insights for understanding the nature of teacher leadership in Jamaica. As I analysed the data, I experienced what Miller and Crabtree (1999) refer to as the many changing rhythms in analysing qualitative data. These, for me, manifested in moments of excitement, as I theorised, reflected and made new discoveries and moments of exasperation as I grappled with theory building from observations made in the data.

The findings presented are reflective of themes that emerged from the data analysis phase. The themes are used to share teacher leaders' perspectives on who they are, what they value, the culture within their school and their agency. As expressed by Miller (2017), the practice of leadership is often culturally situated, hence the ideas presented in this study seek to create a deeper understanding of teacher leadership in a situated context. The study further serves to enhance praxis for teachers, leaders, students and their community, thereby promoting opportunities that should lead to school improvement. This study is limited in its scope to 12 teachers in 12 schools located in six parishes in Jamaica. Therefore, using this study as a starting point, the need exists for other scholars to further the research in this area.

The 12 Teacher Leaders in the Study

The teacher leaders in this study worked in diverse school contexts inclusive of rural and urban dynamics, varying socioeconomic status and varying school types. Their teaching experience ranged from two years to twenty years. Of the twelve teachers, two were male and ten were female. This gender bias towards females is reflective of the national teaching demographic, as there are more female teachers than male teachers in the teaching profession in Jamaica. The participants were assigned pseudonyms to protect their identities. At the time of the study, Nick taught music and was the academic programme representative on the School Board. Tasha was a grade 4 teacher and the staff representative on the school board. Yanique was a grade 2 teacher and curriculum implementation trainer for teachers in grades 1-3 at her school. Sally taught reading as a subject. Lavna was a grade 1 teacher who taught dance as a co-curricular activity to students. Lean was a grade 3 teacher and leader of the Environmental club. Alvernia was a grade 1 teacher. Mark taught technical vocational subjects such as Industrial Techniques and Technical Drawing. Tracey was a Mathematics and Family and Consumer Affairs teacher and a master trainer, certified by the Ministry of education. Grace taught Business Studies subjects and was enrolled in the Aspiring Principals' programme; Sheri was an English teacher and a form teacher. Padna was a teacher of Information Technology and Mathematics. A summary of participants' demographics is provided in table 5.1.

Teacher leadership represents an opportunity to reduce abstract theorising and create change in schools through a deep understanding of the power that resides in shared and distributed leadership (Levin & Schrum, 2016). Six main themes are shared in this study to provide insight into the milieu surrounding teacher leadership in the Jamaican context as expressed by the twelve teacher leaders in the study. These are: (1) characteristics of teacher leaders in Jamaica and what they value; (2) The nexus between principal leadership, school ethos and teacher leadership; (3) the nature of teacher leaders' work; (4) context matters in teacher leaders' work; (5) challenges to teacher leaders' work (6) and agency amidst difficulties. Each theme is discussed using literature interspersed with narratives from the participants to provide a scholarly conversation, give voice to participants' experiences and to bring to life the realities of teacher leadership in Jamaica, thereby providing a situated understanding.

Table 5.1: Demographics of participation

Participant	School type	Location	Years of teaching experience	Qualification	Subject/ grade	Gender
Nick	Secondary	Urban	2	Bachelors	Music	Male
Tasha	Primary	Rural	16	Bachelors	Grade 4	Female
Yanique	Primary	Rural	11	Bachelors	Grade 2	Female
Sally	Primary	Rural	11	Masters	Reading	Female
Lavna	Primary	Rural	9	Masters	Grade 1	Female
Lean	Primary	Urban	12	Masters	Grade 3	Female
Alverine	Primary & Junior High	Urban	10	Masters	Grade 1	Female
Mark	Secondary	Rural	10	Bachelors	Technical Drawing & Industrial Technique	Male
Tracey	Primary & Junior High	Urban	20	Masters	Mathematics & Family and Consumer Affairs	Female
Grace	Primary	Urban	15	Masters	Business Studies	Female
Sheri	Secondary	Urban	6	Masters	English	Female
Padina	Secondary	Rural	9	Bachelors	Information Technology & Mathematics	Female

Characteristics of Teacher Leaders in Jamaica and What They Value

The views from the teacher leaders in the study suggested that they were innovative, had a passion and zeal for people development, were open to learning, self-reflexive in their approach, enthusiastic about their role as a teacher regardless of their circumstances and demonstrated resilience amidst challenges. For example, Sally noted, 'I am more than just a teacher'. While Grace stated, 'I am very determined, so if you say I can't, I will show you why I can'. Interestingly for 50% of the teacher leaders in the study, teaching was not their preferred career choice, but circumstances led them to teaching. However, all participants expressed an altruistic passion and zeal for teaching as a profession once they got started:

> I have always wanted to be a teacher, and family and friends also believed it was a calling. I have always found myself in a position where I was teaching because I love researching and reading. So, me becoming a teacher also came from life experiences and me wanting to be a teacher. (Nick)

> Teaching was not my first passion, but as a result of socioeconomic status, I could not afford the dream career which was law or journalism. So, I went into teaching because this was what I could afford to do. From that experience though, I learnt that what seems to be your passion at first may not be...but you can grow to love it and excel in doing so and this is what has happened with me with teaching. I found my passion accidently and I love it. (Tasha)

The characteristics exhibited by the teacher leaders in this study expanded upon characteristics that international scholars have identified as reflective of teacher leaders (Lumpkin, Claxton, & Wilson, 2014; Danielson, 2006). While articulating their passion and zeal for the profession, teacher leaders also expressed what they valued. Such valuing underpinned their actions and responses to various situations that benefitted self, students, their colleagues and the institution overall. For example, because Yanique valued honesty, self-evaluation and being organised, she engaged in an ongoing examination of herself to derive ways of improving her practice so that her students can benefit:

> I value honesty and evaluating yourself as a teacher. What weaknesses do I have as a teacher and how can I improve on a day-to-

day basis and do the best I can for the students who I have? I believe if you are honest with yourself as a teacher, you should know what is working and what is not and what you can do to improve on what is not working. I also value being organised. I don't think you should be in front of students and not being ready for them; it's not fair to you nor them. (Yanique)

Lean valued humanising her practice through commitment to all. Emanating from Lean's views is also her valuing of social justice as a teacher leader in securing excellence for her school, the school community and by extension her country:

I value standards and I value integrity. I believe whatever you do should speak for itself. If you are a road sweeper you must be the best road sweeper. Your integrity is better kept than recovered. I am passionate about standing up for people, about seeing things in the true way it should be...I believe in excellence. My colleagues know that I am for everybody doing well. I don't like for me to be the only one highlighted. I believe I am that catalyst and I should not be too quick to see my colleagues fail. The other day, a colleague went away on the overseas trained teachers programme and needed videos for her grade one class, and every day I created a video for her because she needed the help. I believe we were all created equal and so we should help each other to do well. I believe we are here to help each other; it's the circle of life. (Lean)

It is the personal internal interrelated domains of commitment and knowledge (Fullan, 1994) expressed by these teacher leaders, coupled with an understanding of their school context and demonstrated through their work to improve student outcomes, that set them apart from other teachers. Furthermore, it is these demonstrated characteristics that will lead to positive effects for the teacher leaders themselves, their colleagues, and, importantly, for their students (Angelle & DeHart, 2016).

When asked why they think they were selected as teacher leaders by their colleagues, the participants' comments reflected statements such as:

'I am always initiating and co-ordinating activities,'

'I offer solutions that usually work,'

'I go the extra mile to ensure students learn,'

'Others see me as genuine in offering help/advice,'

'I am resourceful,'

'I have a good rapport with colleagues, and they are always seeking my advice.'

Interestingly, one participant felt that her teacher leadership role was linked to her institutional knowledge derived from her extended years of service in the same school. As a result of these years of service in the same institution, her colleagues who were junior in years of service looked to her for guidance. Additionally, she was well-respected by parents and her reputation was often used to negotiate conflicts between other teachers and parents or to negotiate privileges between the school and the community. Her comments underscore the view that there are different facets to teacher leadership (York-Barr & Duke, 2004) and there are benefits to be derived from all forms of teacher leadership (Jackson, Burrus, Bassett, & Roberts, 2010). This was what she said:

Being at the school for so long, there are persons at the school or in my grade who come to me for advice even though I am not a senior teacher. I am also co-ordinating activities outside of teaching, so I am always around putting things together. Because I have been at the school for a long time, hence, my opinion is sought on things that those who are new may not know about. Teachers are used as resource persons for each other's class or are invited to planning sessions to share their expertise. My expertise is used frequently at the grade level a lot more than others mainly because I have a longer work experience than the other teachers at that grade level. They tend to think I know more because of this and so they often go with my idea . . . . I recall one day a parent came to argue and she was being boisterous with a teacher who was new. I heard and then went but because the parent knew of me since I have been at the school for a long time, she listened to me and we dealt with the matter in a different way. (Lavna)

Schools are complex institutions propelled by explicit and implicit intentions that cannot be achieved through strict division of roles between administrators and teachers; therefore a shared collaborative approach to leadership is needed (Seltz, 2014). Teacher leaders in the study also expressed that they valued an inclusive and collaborative approach to school improvement, where there are established systems and procedures that are clearly communicated; where staff feel appreciated; where the culture valued autonomy to initiate and where there are opportunities for growth. For such systems, procedures and ethos to exist, the principal in each school must be open to sharing his/her power (Hutton, 2013).

The Nexus Between Principal Leadership, School Ethos and Teacher Leadership

According to Miller (2016), principals by virtue of what they say and do and in how they treat others are the chief custodians of a school's vision and mission and how this is transmitted to those inside and outside the school. The principal's stance, philosophy, leadership style, decision-making approaches and relationship with staff will influence the culture created. Principals help to shape teachers learning, motivation and working conditions. But school culture is not only influenced by the principal, though he or she is the main custodian. The culture of a school is also influenced by the relationships between principal and staff, teachers and teachers, teachers and students, students and students, with parents and with the community. Ensuring that positive relationships exist between the different groups or different levels of leadership in the institution is one of the key roles of the principal. Such relationships are important for creating opportunities to extend leadership. Extending leadership helps the school to make better use of its intellectual and social capital (Harris, 2013; Spillane, 2006). To this end, Conway, Andrews, Jaarsveld and Bauman (2017) argue that in order to bring about school improvement, there is a need to focus on the involvement of a broad range of leaders in creating its culture. More importantly, if principals are to be successful at leading schools in the 21st century, they need to inspire teachers to become leaders and enlist the help of teachers who are leaders.

When teachers see themselves as leaders, their sense of self-efficacy increases, and they become committed to shared goals. This will then translate to increased participation resulting in an influence that is reciprocal for both teacher and principal (Moller & Pankake, 2006; Webb, Neumann, & Jones 2004). However, for reciprocity to occur that benefits the institution, the principal has to act with intentionality in creating the atmosphere that allows teacher leaders to flourish. As argued by Thorton (2016) and Lee-Piggott (2014), the extent to which teacher leadership thrives in any institution is dependent on principal support.

Some teacher leaders in the study expressed various tensions in the relationships amongst the different groups of leaders in their schools. Mark's comment is reflective of such tensions:

> The executive group (principal and vice principal) tend to make harsh decisions without teacher involvement, and because of this, they are not supported by the teachers. They don't listen to the teacher. As a result, students misbehave because they know if teachers make a decision the admin. will overturn it, so they don't bother. For example, teachers will write up a suspension or give students time-out, and the administrative team will overturn that and send the child back to class without consulting the teacher or discussing the matter with teachers. (Mark)

Mark's comments also highlight the need for effective communication between the different levels of leaders in the school to ensure that each group is valued in the decision-making process. School leadership is an art and a science that involves the act of leadership, which is about all that embodies leading, and the actions of leaders, which is about providing leadership (Miller, 2016). Embedded in the nature of school leadership therefore are the burdens that come with school leadership. A principal's lack of understanding and inability to deconstruct these inherent burdens in light of context will result in increased tensions between the principal and his/her staff. Participants in the study expressed various tensions in the relationship between principals and teachers that resulted in a school ethos that was not positive. These were stated as:

- Demonstrated hypocrisy in decision-making by the leader, where staff are made to feel that their views are being listened to but implemented decisions are not reflective of their views. This leads staff with the feeling that they were not really listened to. (Sally, Tracey, Lean, Mark, Sheri, Lavna)

- Gender positioning by males for leadership positions. Participants expressed that because there are such few males and few positions for upward mobility in schools at times, there is a divide in the relationship between the genders, which affects how leadership is enacted. These participants expressed that some males think the females will automatically be selected once there is an opening for a position, and so will try at any cost to outdo the female to get the position. (Tasha, Sally)

- Formation of cliques in large schools. Some participants reported that when the school is large, cliques can form. Where these exist, teachers are afraid to interfere in issues from other departments or across grade levels. This also gives rise to teachers siding with each other, whether or not the result is in the best interest of the institution. (Grace, Lean, Lavna, Tasha, Sally)

Given these views, the onus is on the principal to manage underlying issues through shared leadership and value for teachers' work to create an ethos that facilitates growth for all and maximises the social capital of the institution. Hollingworth, Olsen, Asikin-Garmager and Winn (2018) argue that principals establish positive culture through empowering teachers by cultivating trust, knowing their staff well and engaging in explicit and purposeful communication. Furthermore, maximising the agency that resides in teacher leaders and giving birth to new teacher leaders in an institution is dependent on how well the school principal models the management of relationships as he/she leads. As articulated by Tracey:

I think for you to have effective teacher leadership in an institution, you must have quality leadership for the teachers to look to. There must be proper policies and procedures in place that you follow and not haphazardly as you feel; but protocols for you to follow....It also bears directly on students excelling. An institution can be an institution where children want to go and learn but not where teachers want to go and work, and that I find is bad because it is the teachers in a greater part who will contribute to that environment that stimulates growth and learning. If the leader of a school can tap into the human resources and use those resources not just for the benefit of the institution, but to both the individual and the institution, there is no telling how the institution will grow. (Tracey)

As argued by Dinham (2007), a positive school ethos that promotes positive relationships cannot be achieved without strong school leadership that is authoritative and distributive. An environment that perpetuates negative relationships will not yield the best results from teacher leaders nor give birth to teacher leaders (Scribner & Bradley-Levine, 2010). Such relationships will diminish the work of teacher leaders and create fear and mistrust amongst stakeholders, thereby diminishing the potential for school improvement.

Teacher leaders will flourish in a school culture that reflects democratic ideals, and where the philosophy of shared leadership and the valuing of teachers' work ground the actions of the principal. Padina's comments are reflective of such a culture:

In my school, teachers are right up there with principal. There are some decisions that the principal will have to take as the leader, but we share, and we decide together, and we find that because of that, we don't think about who is leading; we just share an idea and then we work together on it. We are like a family. Most times, he [principal] will ask staff for feedback and ask us to share any challenges we foresee with an idea to be implemented. We don't worry about who is leading, we all work together. For example, if there is an area where a teacher is not comfortable in delivering lessons, teachers normally ask for assistance, especially if they are not comfortable in delivering an area, and we coach each other. Sometimes it's just out of a conversation and especially if I discover something new, we organise sessions to share because we have a sharing culture, and no one feels threatened by anyone. There is no power struggle in our school because we don't separate ourselves; we socialize and show respect to everyone on a professional level. Most times when new staff comes, they are surprised to see us getting along so well. There is just a level of openness even when I came here, where I was coming from, it was not like this. (Padina)

All principals are different and therefore will interpret, act and provide leadership differently. However, increasing the opportunities for teacher leadership increases the support school principals have available and reduces some of the burdens of leadership. For example, where negative relations threaten the school's vision and mission, the teacher leader becomes a critical resource for the principal in building and maintaining a culture that sustains and fosters school improvement. Tasha's comments on leadership and Alverine's comments on the value of teacher leadership in breaking down barriers between the administrative team led by the principal are insightful in this regard:

Leadership makes, and it breaks. The outcome of any great organisation is dependent on the dynamics of the leadership structure. I have seen from experience where leadership has turned institutions that were once dormant into vibrant performing institutions, and I have seen the reverse as a result of poor leadership. (Tasha)

Having a teacher leader who, in the eyes of a teacher, is just a regular person who can't fire you, who is not appraising you or writing you up or putting negatives on your record; having that person tell you that you are not doing something properly and show you what to do will help the person to grow rather, than someone who comes to you and you are afraid of what they will say or do, or you think about what they will put on your appraisal. Teacher leaders enable that kind of growth mindset as far as learning for the teacher is concerned. (Alverine)

Tracey's comment provides guidance on how the Ministry of Education can in turn hold principals accountable for managing and navigating how they lead:

> I think the Ministry of Education needs to look at how they assess school administration. I think teachers should have an important part in assessing who leads them because at the end of the day, nobody knows the leadership like the teachers. You can pop in one day or two and observe and you get a presentation, but when I am there five days per week, there is so much and no more that you can present. (Tracey)

Perhaps prior to the establishment of accountability mechanisms to manage how school principals lead, the need may exist for a shared understanding by principals on the roles of teacher leaders and how the role of teacher leadership corresponds with the overall school organisation (Akert & Martin, 2012).

The Nature of Teacher Leaders' Work

Teacher leaders do not wait to be appointed to a formal role before they offer their expertise to others in order to impact the educational experience of all students and hold the institution to higher levels of achievement (Akert & Martin, 2012). Teacher leaders operate with the desire and commitment to positively influence their colleagues' work with the goal of improving teaching and learning (Bradley-Levine, 2018). From the interviews of the 12 teacher leaders, it can be concluded that teacher leaders' work occupied a position of great influence in their schools. Their influence was with both internal and external stakeholders. However, some schools provided more opportunities for teacher leaders to use such influence without confines, while in others were more restrictive. Where teacher leaders' influence was restricted, it was related to the leadership style of the principal. Nonetheless, though carried out to varying degrees based on school context, teacher leaders in the study expressed that their work entailed some of the following activities:

- Bridging relationship gaps between parents and other teachers

- Serving as representatives for the principal at official functions

- Advocating for students and staff in areas of social welfare and well-being

- Fundraising and soliciting resources to support the work of students and colleagues

- Providing instructional support for effective curriculum implementation

- Providing professional development for colleagues

- Developing and initiating new programmes to benefit students and colleagues

- Forging international teacher networks for soliciting best practices

- Modelling and showcasing evidence-based decision-making

Katzenmeyer and Moller (2001) acknowledged that teacher leaders' work involves three facets: (1) leadership of students and other teachers, (2) leadership of operational tasks and (3) leadership through decision-making or partnerships on committees. The views expressed by the 12 teacher leaders in this study about their work, while not limited to Katzenmeyer and Mollers' categories, can be aligned with the facets they mentioned. The teacher leaders' views about their work also support Danielson's (2006) definition of teacher leaders. For Danielson, teacher leaders are teachers who teach students but also have an influence that goes beyond their own classroom space. She sees their work as one that involves cultivating positive relationships and managing systems and procedures to identify and address problems of teaching and learning. The following narratives provide expressions of the work that teacher leaders perform in their respective schools:

When I just came to the school, the students were performing poorly on the literacy and numeracy tests and within each year, I would surpass the target that the Ministry of Education sets for the school. This is because I have implemented things in this school that persons felt could not be done. I have received a number of awards for these things. I am now a motivational speaker. Persons who I don't know would hear of my work and request me to speak at a graduation or parenting seminar, and my principal sometimes asks me to represent him at functions. Overall, I am a leader based on my rapport with my colleagues, students and parents. (Sally)

I always try to ensure that teachers understand certain concepts. I also try to ensure that there is a sense of responsibility where I think I must lead to ensure that all my colleagues are on par with what's happening in the grade. I am at a school where we have four of each grade levels, and I think it is rather unfair for me to find all these creative activities and do them with my students when there are three other classes that can benefit. There are times when I take it upon myself to have grade meetings and share with the teachers what I have tried in my classroom and how it worked. I try to encourage my colleagues to try it too, and then let's have a post meeting to share the results on how well it has gone and whether it is something that we should continue. (Alverine)

I can't say I get up to lead because of teacher leadership. I think I lead because I can't be bothered with foolishness. I just like to get things done. Some of the big things I have gone out to do like: getting over $700,000 in funding, refurbishing the security post, getting a welfare programme started to feed some children, beg computers, beg printers, etc. Maybe it is just because I am frustrated, I have put things together to do things. I am just someone who will get up and say we are going to do something, and I put a team together and put things together. They are always selecting me to do things. They are always coming to me with their problems. If anyone comes from the outside, they do not go to the vice principal; they find me to represent the school. (Grace)

The teacher leaders also expressed that they possessed expertise in different areas. This was demonstrated in different ways and was context and task dependent. Their expertise was demonstrated through their content knowledge level on different subject matter, ability to be organised, ability to motivate and inspire, ability to manage or manipulate systems, documentation and record keeping skills, ability to collaborate, data use to support initiatives or their ability to generate solutions. No one teacher leader possessed all these skills, but what was common among the teacher leaders was their ability to initiate, mobilise and galvanise support for whatever mission they had to accomplish. This helped to set them apart from other teachers. Additionally, whatever expertise they possessed these were used to benefit the institution:

> Teachers are often coming to me for ideas, especially ideas on record keeping and how to capture more data to help their students because this is what I do. I capture data to help my students. I am not a senior teacher, but I was asked to supervise teachers in grades 1-3 because of my demonstrated knowledge in how to use the curriculum. The teachers come to me for planning, strategies, record keeping, collecting data, and I have been invited to other schools to do sessions for them as well. (Yanique)

Tasha relays a story which cements the nature of teacher leaders' work and how teacher leaders use the influence they possess to benefit the school. Her story also highlights the need for mutual trust between principal and teacher leader and teacher leader and his or her colleagues for teacher leaders' work to thrive. Trust must be evident in order to make the best use of the teacher leader's expertise. The principal must trust the teacher leader to function in the way he or she sees best to mobilise staff, and the teacher leader must trust the principal to believe in him or her regardless of the outcome so that he or she can do whatever it takes to mobilise staff. Additionally, the teacher leader's colleague must be able to trust him or her to remain true to his or her word and to lead by example:

> There is a situation that stands out in my mind. In the past, we have had a club in the institution that was dubbed the social club.

This club would take care of the welfare of the staff in terms of having excursions for staff or financial needs. There was a change in management in terms of principal and so the club became defunct because of internal wrangling. The principal that came on board really wanted to get it up and running and so in a sense, it was proving difficult. Because I knew of the benefits from this club, one day I walked into the principal's office and asked him if he would like me to assist in getting this club operational again, and he said to go ahead, and without any further instructions, he just allowed me to do what needed to be done. So, I went back to my group and constructed my committee and told him of the persons I would approach to lead the club and asked if he was okay with them. He was wondering if persons were going to help because it failed before. I told him to leave it to me. I then held the committee meetings and we decided on the mission and vision of the club, then I did an internal memo and took it around personally to each member of staff to promote the plans and the requirements to be a member, which also included paying fees. Every single member of staff agreed to sign up, even the ones who were withdrawn previously signed up for it and the club to date has been operational for five years. Through this club and its committee, I am able to plan trips to take the teachers to all-inclusive hotels, and establish various initiatives and we continue have a vibrant social club. (Tasha)

Tasha gave another example of the nature of her work as a teacher leader:

In addition to being a trained teacher, I am a trained guidance counselor, and so advocacy is part of what I do and I have interest in social work. I abhor seeing injustice. For example, when students come to school and they are not properly attired. They appear to have not had proper meals and are being exposed to abuse. Usually I am the one who is trying to find out from them what is happening, referring them to the guidance counsellor, etc. I give a hug and if necessary call the parents. There was even one point where I literally adopted a child for Christmas. I took the child home and ensured the child was properly fed and had the requisite resources to have a better educational experience, and that ended in that child being the first from the community to be placed at a traditional high school. (Tasha)

Context Matters in Teacher Leaders' Work

It is widely acknowledged by various scholars that context matters in leadership (Miller, 2017; Dorfman et al., 1997), and this is no different for teacher leaders' work. Teacher leaders' work may be expressed differently based on contextual variations. The teacher leaders' work in this study differed based on school size, community characteristics and geographic location. Two examples are provided here to showcase how context shaped teacher leaders' actions. The examples also highlight how teacher leaders empowered students to see beyond their immediate circumstances/contexts.

An excerpt from Mark

Mark, a teacher in a rural secondary school, describes an encounter that required him to demonstrate an understanding of his context and to act based on what the context required. Mark's story also re-iterates the importance of shared leadership in school and the importance of teacher leaders.

> In this community, these students don't even go out, they don't even know Kingston. They are not exposed. I try to get them exposed and if I don't do that to help them, the cycle will continue, and they will become criminals. Because I live in the community, I wouldn't want to know that my own students robbed me. I live in the community, so I cannot give up on them. I have no plans to go to any other country. Jamaica is a paradise.

> Ninety percent of my leadership and power is to motivate students and I get to do anything I want to do with them. No matter how bad a boy or girl is, I always give them a smile. Once things go wrong, I let them sit for a while and then after I try to teach morals through it.

There was this young man who had extremely irregular attendance, sometimes once for the week or twice or three times he would show up, never the full week. I investigated to find out what was his situation. He would come to school with the deodorant marks showing on his shirt. This was very thick and sticky looking. His clothes were very dirty and he was smelly. So, one day I said to him, 'You remain after class because I want to talk to you'. So, after everyone left, I said to him that I noticed he had been absent frequently and I asked why. He said at times he was absent because he had to be on the farm with his dad and he did not have enough shirts and pants. I told him to take one of his shirts to me the next day. He was curious as to why, but I told him to just take it. He did the next day and I took it home for him and washed and ironed it and gave it to him. I asked him what he noticed about the shirt and he said it was clean. So, I proceeded to ask him about certain parts like the collar and arm and the difference between the shirt he gave me and the one now. I then proceeded to tell him and ask him about myself and how I come to school with my clothes and whether he has ever seen me looking dirty. I then told him to take the other shirt he had for me the next day and I took it home and did the same thing (washed and ironed it). Then on the weekend I bought him two new shirts and pants and from that day on, he has been with me. He said I am his father because everything he would have needed at school, I would provide for him until he graduated. He also had problems with reading, so I had my wife who is a teacher to assist him with reading and then I brought in the reading teacher. We basically started working with him in all subjects. He then started doing so well in school and his average moved from 30s to 60s. We would give him writing tasks and he would complete them. He was very willing to learn as well. (Mark)

Embedded in Mark's story is the ability of the teacher leader to see the bigger picture and an understanding of his/her role in transforming society. This speaks to a conceptualisation of a leader regardless of the level at which he/she operates as a visionary, one who commits to the goals of the vison while enjoining others to seek a better future (Bush, 2018). Patriotism to country and community motivated Mark to take actions for his students who could not do better because of their circumstances. Mark's story also highlights the need for teacher leaders to understand that they are role models for their students and therefore must set examples that will show students the way to self-liberation. Another critical issue highlighted by Mark's story is the co-operative, collaborative support that is needed in schools to aid the development of the whole child.

An excerpt from Lean

Lean works in an urban primary and junior high school. In her school context, many of her students are from inner-city communities located near the school. Lean describes her students as being from resource challenged communities. As such, the school needs to offer respite and be a refreshing environment that helps students to see beyond their immediate circumstances and develop their intellectual abilities (Hudley, 2013). Additionally, embedded in Lean's narrative is the fact that teacher leaders need to demonstrate an understanding of their social context by deconstructing the issues that students face and deriving solutions.

> The students come with their own knowledge of things and how things operate, and you know the classroom requires a formal setting. The whole surrounding can be depressing. We go up to grade 9 and there are things that surprise you as a teacher. Children getting home very late at nights. Children taking illegal weapons to school and I don't believe my environment cultivates a culture of excelling. Take for example a child in the last staging of GSAT [the primary exit examination at the time of the study) who went to be awarded by the government because she got high scores and she was placed at a top traditional high school, and this was not something that was highlighted in the school as a big thing or a *wow* moment. Instead an event with a magician was what was highlighted, and when the child came back with her mom, nothing was said. It was all about the magician show. I saw the video of the event with the child receiving the award as someone posted it and I was saying to

myself that this should have been shared with the student body and let them feel inspired. At my school they have songs, and these are the songs the students hear in their community, so one day I decided to suggest to the teacher who operates the system, can't you change the music? Let us change what the children listen to let school be a refreshing place. I met with the teachers of mathematics, home and family life education, etc. I said to them, 'People outside must always be wondering what is happening at school because it is the same things the children sing in the community. You have heritage, Jamaica Day, etc. You use the same songs they are used to in their communities which for me they have no meaning, they cannot inspire the students to do better'. So, we all agreed and changed the music to ones with softer tones and music that are age appropriate. I got different songs to be played. I have seen now where the children are learning new songs. In the morning I now get them to listen to soothing soft music to set the tone for the day. In setting the tone, they need a calm spirit because if they already get wound up outside {in their communities}, already it is very hard to get them calm. You wouldn't like to know the influence the music has on the brain, so now all teachers bring something different in terms of music to the children. Because of the students' environment we have to bring something different to the children . . . . For example, I will say to a colleague, 'You know I heard you this morning speaking over the microphone to the children and I don't think next time you should use that tone and approach because the children are used to that in their community'. I said to her, 'Remember you were on the microphone and you have to remember that people all the way out the road could hear you; you have to talk to them in a better tone and use language that is more respectful and friendlier while being firm. Remember you are an educator'. (Lean)

Mark and Lean's narratives give rise to two critical aspects of teacher leaders' roles, that of achieving both emotional and cognitive justice for students. Emotional justice is about tapping into the feelings that students come with, valuing the humanness, and the potential that resides in students despite their backgrounds, and helping students to use negative feelings associated with their circumstances as opportunities for empowerment. Cognitive justice is about helping students to understand that despite seemingly low levels of academic achievement, they possess knowledge that is useful, that is worthwhile knowing and that their knowledge is important for the functioning of other students. It also means showing students how to use the knowledge they possess to empower themselves and others around them. In this sense, cognitive justice is about the diversity of knowledge and the equality of the knower (Visvanatha, 2007). In the current context of schooling in Jamaica where disparities exist and a perpetuation of classism and classification strives based on types of schools and geographical location of schools, cognitive justice will not be achieved without emotional justice. Hence the teacher leaders' role is important in helping students achieve both forms of justice, thereby positioning the teacher leader at the heart of the learning relationships among the different groups of school stakeholders (Gunter, 2016).

Challenges to Teacher Leaders' Work

With determination, teacher leaders carry out their work to make a difference for both their internal and external stakeholders. Notwithstanding this determination, the teacher leaders in the study expressed that they faced various challenges as they carried out their work. Two of such challenges included school politics, which at times resulted in a culture of segregation, and the effects on students from lack of financial resources available to their parents to meet their learning needs.

School politics and segregation

For Tracey, Sally, Grace, Alverine, Mark, Lavna, Sheri and Lean, a culture of staff segregation and a clan-like approach in making decisions at their schools was one of their biggest challenges. Challenges such as these will give rise to various forms of tensions and marginalisation of teachers and principals, which will affect the ways in which teacher leaders are identified and treated and the work they are able to perform (Wenner & Campbell, 2017). These eight teacher leaders felt that there were those teachers in their schools who just followed whatever the principal said just to ensure that he/she got ahead. Grace described as belonging to the 'backra master' (slave master) mentality where teachers follow the leader without independently thinking or interrogating the leader's decision for themselves. Schools in the 21st century are even more complex than the previous century as diversity has increased. In order to ensure equity and fairness for all, independent yet collaborative thinking is needed to challenge issues of injustice wherever they exist. A 'backra master' approach is therefore self-serving, is not in the best interest of those they are required to serve and results in the leader exploiting the teachers. Additionally, these eight teacher leaders described the clan like approach as one where teachers are organised around a similar interest and as a result share a close-knit relationship. From the data examined, shared interests may be along subject department lines, belonging to a grade, or belonging to the religious group that established the school. In such situations, as a member of the clan you are protected by the clan and your actions are not influenced by those outside the clan.

But clan in these eight schools was not limited to teachers and teachers, but also extended to the principal and those who belonged to his/her inner circle. As members of this inner circle, their authority and influence were sanctioned by the principal. They possessed knowledge of decisions to be made by the principal ahead of staff meetings, as the principal usually enlisted their support with the general staff prior to meetings. The eight teacher leaders expressed that as a member of the inner circle loyalty resides with the principal regardless of the consequences of the decision. Furthermore, no matter how excellent an idea was if one did not belong to the inner circle, it would not get implemented. Nonetheless, the passion and purpose that characterised teacher leaders work, allowed them to find ways to navigate such obstacles in their schools. For example, teacher leaders navigated these obstacles by collaborating with persons who belonged to the clan and using members of the clan to promote the idea as if it was theirs, just to ensure that the idea was given due attention.

Sheri, who worked in a rural secondary school with strong religious affiliation, shared this:

> There is a particular culture in my school where sometimes I do not
> believe some teachers are treated fairly. My school is an Anglican

institution and sometimes I believe that they look out for their people even though some of these persons do not have the best interest of the school and students at heart, but because of their whole religious aspect they are given specialty treatment. I do not think that it is fair, so sometimes persons are given roles because of that and those that are deserving of the position or the title are ignored because of the culture....Sometimes you will have some teachers who will talk about the situation but for some people, it is neither here nor there for them. (Sheri)

Tracey, who worked in an urban primary and junior high school, shared a more detailed perspective on segregation as she compares how schools operate with her previous job in the private sector:

There are many different cultures at my school. Based on who you are and what you stand for, you will experience different things. For me I am strictly a professional person. I was trained in the private sector and I cannot see myself doing or acting in a certain way. I think the culture at my school is one that prevents you from growing if you have a voice and if you make your voice be heard. It's a culture that confuses you. I think the institution practises a lot of politics and it prevents the growth of the institution itself in the way you would love for it to grow for you to say the institution is truly becoming what it can, what it can become. If you have a voice and you make it heard, you are blacklisted. It is like a glass ceiling right above your head; if you pretend you don't see and if you go along with the status quo, then life would be different. For me that is hard because of how I was trained and how I think as a person I should operate, and so I did not just allow myself to be baptised in the culture of this institution. I observe and I speak out, even if it has nothing to do with me because I always think that not because it has nothing to do with me doesn't mean I should not say anything because I don't know if tomorrow the same thing that I turned a blind eye to today could become the thing that prevents me tomorrow. So, I always look at the greater good and not just self. It is about my genuine sense of care for the organisation. For me after much observation and taking into consideration all that I have learnt as a manager, the administration is the greatest setback because of politics....Administration is the greatest setback and for me because of the culture I do not see it changing. I look to colleagues outside the institution for support. When you feel you can't, they will show you why you can or help you to find a reason why not to give in. (Tracey)

Lean, in offering a perspective, likened the segregation in her school to that of two political parties.

We have two types of staff at my school. We have a staff that was hired by the outgoing principal and a staff that was hired by the current principal, and there is no collegiality amongst the two groups across the board, but the staff that was there before; they tend to have that collegiality, a more closely-knitted bond. Because of the divide you find that the students' best interest is not at the forefront. So even if you have a best piece of information that could better help me as a teacher to do something more creative, there is no sharing if you are not in my group. I think the current principal has a new teachers' induction meeting where she would indoctrinate the new staff regarding the old staff and because of that they do not want to interface with you because in their mind, they know what it is already. If they are talking to a member of the old staff and they see the principal coming, they would move away. So, when that happens you don't have collegiality and so there is no common goal. It's like we have two political parties and we have two different parliaments and at no given time are we on the same page, and until these children become the forefront of what we are doing and put self aside, we won't have the desired results. For example, I might see something on your chalkboard and it's not written properly, and I will say to another person to go tell her that her chart needs to be fixed. I wouldn't tell her because it won't be received in a way of no ill intentions, so it's like a battlefield. (Lean)

Though teacher leaders found solutions to the challenges, it must be understood that practices of segregation result in entrenchment of 'othering' in schools. Such 'othering' can negatively influence school improvement, as a great idea that could benefit the school may reside with someone who is excluded from the group and who may not be bothered to ensure it gets implemented regardless. As teacher leaders carry out their work, they must be critically conscious of issues linked to unequal power distribution in schools (Bradley-Levine, 2018).

The effects on students from lack of financial resources

For the teacher leaders in this study, lack of resources to support the work they do was linked to the low socio-economic status of students and the homes and communities from which they came. Thompson (2018) concurs as she notes that these inequities from students' homes translate to the inequities at school. Poverty was a real issue with which the teacher leaders in some schools had to confront. They also noted that, lack of resources due to students' low socioeconomic status had a ripple effect on students. This was evident in students' unpreparedness for class and their ongoing low performance, which then resulted in their lack of confidence as learners. In a report from OECD (2016) on students who participated in PISA, they concluded that 'while many disadvantaged students succeed at school … socioeconomic status is associated with significant differences in performance as advantaged students tend to outscore their disadvantaged peers by large margins' (p. 214). In sharing how students socio-economic background influenced the work she performed as a teacher leader, Yanique and Tasha noted:

> The things that make my work difficult is the students being unprepared; they also lack confidence. Their confidence level tends to be very low because some of them have been failing for so long, so I have to spend most of my time trying to build their confidence and giving them things to make them succeed in bits, so they can try harder having seen their little successes. Another challenge is that sometimes the students come to school hungry, dirty, and that is hard for me as a teacher. Not having the supplies that they need to

learn and then I have to provide the resources and I have to tend to these issues before learning can take place. (Yanique)

My work is made more difficult because of the socio-economic status of the community and the composition of the neighborhood. It is difficult to get students with the requisite experience and resources that would enhance the process of teaching and learning. Parental guidance and support are challenging given its location; many of the students who are often challenged by reading you find that their parents are from the lower socio-economic status and it's difficult to get parents on board to participate. Students don't come with resources, have nutritional deficiencies, limited experiences and financial challenges. (Tasha)

Sally explains how she helps the students who experience financial challenges:

I get financial resource support for the students. I get assistance from the school to provide for the needs of the students, especially where parents do not have lunch money for the children. Once I know and ask the school, I will get the support and so I can call the parent and say send the child to school because he/she will get lunch. (Sally)

However, Alverine, felt that despite lacking financial resources some parents did not value education:

The other challenge I have with them is the lack of provision of material for the students. You find that parents don't really see the need of education, and so they often times prefer to spend their money on themselves rather than ensuring their children have the things they need for school. Some parents seem to have their own ideas of how things should be.

Furthermore, some teacher leaders felt that despite the low socio-economic status of some parents, they could show more support for their children through attending and participating in school activities. Notwithstanding these views on how parents could do better, these issues faced by the teacher leaders are social justice related issues and need a combination of strategies to include a co-operative collaborative partnership between school, home and community. Social justice issues are complex and require multi-sectoral actions to address. King recognises this when he stated in a UNICEF (2018) report on the situational analysis of the education sector in Jamaica, that the 'competing demands of various social issues for limited attention and even more limited resources is the clichéd headache of social policy-making' (p. 5). The government of Jamaica has sought to address some of these issues through development and implementation of policies such as increasing school resource allocation, increasing support for parental involvement in schools among others (UNICEF, 2018). However, the views from these teacher leaders suggest that much more is needed.

Agency Amidst Difficulties

Teacher leaders are active, innovative and collegial members of staff. They possess a deep sense of purpose and a passion that propels that purpose. The context and culture of their schools both internal and external may enable or inhibit that passion. In instances where the culture of their school sought to inhibit that passion, with their depth of understanding of their responsibility to self and others they embraced such responsibility and forged ahead to achieve agency. The nature of the teacher leaders in this study indicated that above all else they were able to achieve agency for self and for others. Agency for self was underpinned by first valuing self (who am I?). Such valuing of self led to a philosophy that echoed statements such as the one echoed by Mark, 'I am not just a teacher' and another echoed by Nick, 'I believe if you are a teacher it is important for you to see yourself as a leader and understand the responsibility that comes with that'. Achieving agency for others was underpinned by a desire to achieve justice for all and by what Tasha termed an 'abhorrence of injustice'. This meant that they became what Tracey termed 'voice for the voiceless and those colleagues who would whisper'. The descriptions by the teachers align with the views of scholars who argue that teacher leadership is not a set of behaviours, but a state of being (Wenner & Campbell, 2016; Collison, 2012).

As the teacher leaders in this study carried out their work at various schools, their tenets of agency included a demonstrated understanding of their context, an ability to negotiate objectively during periods of tension, valuing the work of their colleagues and using data as evidence to support initiative or decision-making (Priestly, Biesta, & Robinson, 2015). Their stories, however, only represent a snapshot of what their work involved and their agentic role.

I live by empowering me. I live by my word and so if I can't do it, I will tell you. I believe whatever you do, should speak for itself. If you are a road sweeper you must be the best road sweeper. Your integrity is better kept than recovered. I am passionate about standing up for people, about seeing things in the true way that it should be. However, I have now realised that not because I see things one way it means others are going to see it the same way, but I believe I can help them to see it. (Lean)

You have to understand the politics and know how to navigate it to initiate and implement ideas; don't get involved in it....I advocate for the children all the while and sometimes for the teachers too. For example, I am the face of begging in order to get help for the teachers and the school. One of the things I did for example was to find out why the teachers at my school were frustrated. The answer was, too much paperwork. The elder VP is into paperwork. She doesn't even like when you type things and give to her and because of that they have a lot of hand-written things; that's why they are frustrated. So, what I did specifically to aid the teachers is that all the documents they would have to write on I did a soft copy and emailed it to them. I also developed a report system with Excel so they can automatically generate report. They don't have to add up anything. So instead of taking three days to do a report, they can do it in half an hour. I got all teachers signed up for a computer class training and even the VP went. They used to complain about printing. I went to a company to seek sponsorship and I got it and I bought a printer so that teachers can have access to print. (Grace)

My passion is literacy and getting the students to be able to read. When I came to the school, there was not much data on the students for me to help the students and how the child was progressing. Though we knew the literacy level was about 13%, there was no formal reading diagnostic done....I got the school to start collecting data for each student for each year and follow up each student to see if he/she is growing and how we can help each student. I realised from the groups that I have joined through social media that develop routine for these students is very essential to them being able to pick up quickly. So, every year I talk about it in staff meetings. I volunteer to do sessions with staff on developing routines. I tried out the strategies on how to develop routine for the students, collected the data and presented it to the school. I got other teachers to try it out in another grade and I monitor to ensure teachers are doing what we decided, and I share the results with the Ministry of Education. We followed them from grades 1-3 and we see where it has worked for the three years with the students, and they were able to make connections with their previous grades. (Yanique)

Alvarine's comments also indicated that the administrative team had a role to play in helping teachers to achieve agency. This is what she stated:

In schools oftentimes, teachers are afraid of administration and they believe that whatever negative view administration have of them, it can be used against them and they can lose their jobs and so this cripples teachers' autonomy. . . . I think teachers should not be made to feel afraid of administration because I believe that although you are a trained teacher, you can still grow so whatever mistakes you make, you need to learn from them. (Alvarine)

The perspectives shared by the teacher leaders here suggest that being a teacher leader in these schools embodied varied roles, was organic and was not an easy undertaking for these teachers. For these teachers to have assumed these roles amidst such difficulties suggest that teacher leadership can be practised by any teacher, any time and in any context (Hunzicker, 2017). It therefore means that while systems and procedures are needed to fuel their passion and drive, equally, systems and procedures must be in place to protect them from teacher leader 'burn out'. Amidst the implementation of recent (2016) ongoing curriculum reforms in schools in Jamaica, more teacher leaders need to emerge in schools to help principals lead these reform initiatives.

References

Angelle, P. S., & DeHart, C. A. (2016). Comparison and evaluation of four models of teacher leadership, *Research in Educational Administration & Leadership, 1*(1), 85–119.

Akert, N & Martin, B.N. (2012). The role of teacher leaders in school improvement through the perceptions of principals and teachers. *International Journal of Education,* 4(4), 284–299. https://doi.org/10.5296/ije.v4i4.2290

Bradley-Levine, J. (2018). Advocacy as a Practice of Critical Teacher Leadership. *International Journal of Teacher leadership,* 9(1), 47–62.

Bush, T. (2018). Transformational leadership: Exploring common conceptions. *Educational Management Administration and Leadership,* 46(6), 883–887.

Clandinin, D. J., & Connelly, F. M. (1992). Teacher as curriculum maker. In P. Jackson (Ed.), *Handbook of curriculum research* (pp. 363–401). New York: MacMillan.

Conway, J., Andrews, D., Jaarsveld, L., and Bauman, C. (2017). [AU: the title of the chapter appears to be missing here] In P. Miller (Ed.) *Cultures of educational leadership.* London: Palgrave MacMillan.

Collinson, V. (2012). Leading by earning, learning by leading. *Professional Development in Education,* 38(2), 247–266.

Creswell, J. (2012). *Qualitative inquiry and research design: Choosing among five approaches.* London: Sage Publishing.

Danielson, C. (2007). The many faces of leadership. *Educational Leadership,* 65(1), 14–19.

Danielson, C. (2006). *Teacher leadership that strengthens professional practice.* Alexandria, VA: Association for Supervision and Curriculum Development.

Dinham, S. (2007). Authoritative Leadership, Action Learning and Student Accomplishment. Retrieved from https://research.acer.edu.au/research_conference_2007/3

Dorfman, W., Howell, P., Hibbino, S., Lee, K., Tate, U., & Bautista, A. (1997). Leadership in Western and Asian countries: commonalities and differences in effective leadership processes across cultures. *The Leadership Quarterly,* 8 (3), 233–274.

Fullan, M. G. (1994). Teacher leadership: A failure to conceptualize. In D. R. Wall-
    ing (Ed.), *Teachers as leaders* (pp. 241–253). Bloomington, IN: Phi Delta
    Kappa Educational Foundation.

George, N., Henry-Wilson, M., & Plunkett, N. (2016). A case study in Jamaica's re-
    form of teacher education: Preparing teachers for the 21st century classroom.
    In C. Gentles Hordatt *ICET 2016, 60th world assembly 60th yearbook of
    teacher education.* School of Education. Mona, Kingston: UWI.

Gunter, H. (2016). Teacher leadership challenges and opportunities, pp. 114–123.
    Retrieved from http://citeseerx.ist.psu.edu/viewdoc/download?doi=10.1.1.528.
    5736&rep=rep1&type=pdf

Harris, A. (2013). Distributed leadership: Friend or foe. *Educational Management
    Administration and Leadership, 30*(2), 95–110.

Holingworth, L., Olsen, D., Asikin-Garmager, A, & Winn, K. (2018). Initiating
    conversations and opening doors: How principals establish a positive build-
    ing culture to sustain school improvement efforts. *Educational Management
    Administration and Leadership, 46*(6) 1014–1034.

Hudley, C. (2013). Education and urban schools. American Psychological Associa-
    tion. Retrieved from https://www.apa.org/pi/ses/resources/indicator/2013/05/
    urban-schools

Hunzicker, J. (2017). From teacher to teacher leader: A conceptual model. *Interna-
    tional Journal of Teacher Leadership, 8*(2), 1–27.

Hutton, D. (2013). High-performing Jamaican Principals: Understanding their
    passion, commitment and abilities. In Miller, P. *School leadership in the
    Caribbean: Perceptions, practices paradigms.* United Kingdom, Symposium
    Books.

Jackson, T., Burrus, J., Bassett, K., & Roberts, R. (2010). *Teacher leadership: An
    assessment framework for an emerging area of professional practice.* Princ-
    eton, New Jersey: Center for New Constructs, ETS.

Katzenmeyer, M., & Moller, G. (2001). *Awakening the sleeping giant: Helping
    teachers develop as leaders.* Thousand Oaks, CA: Corwin Press.

Lee-Pigott, R, (2014). When teachers lead: An analysis of teacher leadership in one
    primary school. *Caribbean Curriculum, 22,* 105–132.

Levin, B., & Schrum, L. (2016). *Every teacher a leader: Developing the needed
    dispositions, knowledge, and skills for teacher leadership.* Thousand Oaks,
    CA: Corwin Press.

Lumpkin, A., Claxton, H., & Wilson, A. (2014). Key characteristics of teacher
    leaders in schools. *Administrative Issues Journal, 4*(2), 59–67.

Miller, P. W. (2017). *Cultures of educational leadership: Global and intercultural
    perspectives* Basingstoke, UK: Palgrave Macmillan.

Miller, P. (2016). *Exploring school leadership in England and the Caribbean: New
    insights from a comparative approach.* London: Bloomsbury Academic.

Miller, W., Crabtree, B. (1999). Clinical research: a multimethod typology and qual-
    itative roadmap. In Crabtree B, Miller W (eds). Doing aQualitative Research,
    2nd edn. London: Sage.

Moller, G., & Pankake, A. (2006). *Lead with me: A principal's guide to teacher
    leadership.* New York: Eye on Education.

National Education Inspectorate Report. (2015). Chief Inspector's Baseline Report 2015. Retrieved from http://www.nei.org.jm/Portals/0/Content/Documents/Chief%20Inspector's%20Baseline%20Report%202015.pdfer=2016-06-23-130247-730

OECD, (2016). PISA2015 results. Excellence and Equity in Education (Volume 1). Retrieved from https://read.oecd-ilibrary.org/education/pisa-2015-results-volume-i_9789264266490-en#page1

Priestly, M., Biesta, G., Robinson, S. (2015). *Teacher agency: An ecological approach.* Bloomsbury. London.

Scribner, J. S., & Bradley-Levine, J. (2010). The meaning(s) of teacher leadership in an urban high school reform. *Educational Administration Quarterly, 46*(4), 491–522. Retrieved from http://dx.doi.org/10.1177/0013161X10383831

Seltz, J. (2014). Teacher leadership: The what, the why, and the how of teachers as leaders Retrieved from http://www.ascd.org/ASCD/pdf/siteASCD/wholechild/fall2014wcsreport.pdf

Silva, D. Y., Gimbert, B., & Nolan, J. (2000). Sliding the doors: Locking and unlocking possibilities for teacher leadership. *Teachers College Record, 102*(4), 779–804.

Spillane, J. (2006). *Distributed leadership.* San Francisco, CA: Jossey-Bass.

Strauss, A., & Corbin, J. (1998). *Basics of qualitative research: Grounded theory procedures and techniques* (2nd ed.). Newbury Park, CA: Sage.

Thomson, S. (2018). Achievement at school and socioeconomic background—an educational perspective, editorial. *Science of Learning, 3*(5), 1–2. Retrieved from https://www.nature.com/articles/s41539-018-0022-0.pdf

Thorton, H. (2016). Excellent teachers leading the way: How to cultivate teacher leadership. In Blair, E. (Ed.). *Teacher Leadership: The new foundations of teacher education* (pp. 88–96, 2nd ed.). New York. Peter Lang.

UNICEF (2018). Situation Analysis of Jamaican Children-2018. Retrieved from https://www.unicef.org/jamaica/UNICEF_20180618_SituationAnalysis_web.pdf

University of Technology. (2015). "Needs analysis and front-end analysis to support improved quality assurance in teachers' colleges and community colleges offering teacher training in Jamaica." Kingston, Jamaica: Office of Curriculum Development and Evaluation, University of Technology.

Visvanatha, S. 2007. Between cosmology and system: The heuristics of a dissenting imagination. In B. de Sousa Santos (Ed.), *Anpicother knowledge is possible: Beyond Northern epistemologies* (pp. 182–218). London: Verso.

Webb, P. T., Neumann, M., & Jones, L. C. (2004). Politics, school improvement, and social justice: A triadic model of teacher leadership. *The Educational Forum, 68*(3), 254–262. Retrieved from http://dx.doi.org/10.1080/00131720408984637

Yin, R. (2011). *Doing qualitative research from start to finish.* New York: Guilford Press.

York-Barr, J., & Duke, K. (2004). What do we know about teacher leadership? Findings from two decades of scholarship. *Review of Educational Research, 74,* 255–316.

Holingworth, L., Olsen, D., Asikin-Garmager, A, Winn, K. (2018). Initiating conversations and opening doors: How principals establish a positive building culture to sustain school improvement efforts. *Educational Management Administration and Leadership, 46*(6), 1014–1034.

Weiner, J. & Campbell, T. (2017). The theoretical and empirical basis of teacher leadership: A review of the literature. *Review of Educational Research. 87*(1), 134–171.

CHAPTER SIX

Reflections, Implications and Conclusions

CARMEL ROOFE

THE TEACHER LEADERS IN the study exhibited actions that were seen and experienced by everyone around them. Despite the varying school types within which these teacher leaders worked, it is evident that all 12 teacher leaders possessed competencies and experience that they utilised to benefit both internal and external stakeholders of their schools. From the study, the key characteristics exhibited by these teacher leaders can be summed up in what I call the ZRESS character (See figure 6). The following is an explanation of the ZRESS character depicted by teacher leaders in the study.

Z- Their views suggested they were zealous about the teaching profession and how it can contribute to a purpose bigger than self.

R- Resilient and resourceful. They knew how to use human and material resources to address identified needs. They were resilient despite circumstances.

E- They were eager to learn and therefore participated in self-directed ongoing professional development and networking opportunities that could improve their capacity to aid their learners and the institution.

S- They were self-evaluative as they were constantly critiquing self to sharpen skills or improve self in relation to profession or role so that they are effective in meeting the needs of those they were serving.

S- Solutions oriented. The teachers in the study were self-starters as they sought solutions for problems that emerged. They were agentic in their roles as they were initiators of solutions without being prompted or led.

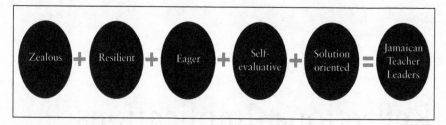

Figure 6.1: Chacteristics of Jamaican teacher leaders in the study

In addition to the characteristics exhibited by the teacher leaders in the study, it was evident that they were led by a core set of values and principles that guided their actions as they sought to achieve cognitive, emotional and social justice for all. These core principles and values allowed them to establish good rapport with colleagues, students and their leaders, regardless of their contextual variations. The teacher leaders in the study therefore underscore the belief that teacher leaders possess the ethos needed to influence the whole learner and their colleagues towards positive development and can therefore serve as positive role models for students and peers. Having these teachers in any school should be the catalyst for ongoing professional development, especially when new reforms are implemented in schools.

Insights for Principal Leadership and Teacher Leadership

Of note from this study is the shared perspective by the teacher leaders about the role of the school principal in fostering a school culture that enables or inhibits the work of teacher leaders. School principals need to guard against staff segregation and practices of othering and manage school politics so that it does not negatively affect school improvement. Additionally, while the principal must promote a spirit of co-operation and collaboration, he/she must be sensitive to the potential harm that could arise when teams begin to bond and begin to form alliances that are not constructive nor open to the views and reasoning of others outside the group. As the principal, he/she must be objective and utilise skills appropriate to relationship and team building to prevent the negatives that can be derived from collaborative work to overshadow the benefits. Conversely, the teacher leader must never find him/herself embroiled in negative school politics as this will diminish positive influence and perpetuate negative influence or modelling, thus inhibiting progress for self, others and the institution. Furthermore, birthing new teacher leaders will occur best in situations that are open, honest, collegial and have clearly established protocols and mechanisms for communication and actions.

The energy that teacher leaders possess requires a principal who is confident in his/her skills and abilities to lead, as lack of confidence will result in the principal feeling as if the teacher leader wants to assume his/her position. Teacher leaders have a deep desire to see situations improve and they are fueled by this desire, hence their actions at times may be misinterpreted. Findings from teacher leaders in this study who expressed views about their principal's role in fostering segregation begs certain questions, such as: Who will protect the teacher leader when the principal does not appreciate that the teacher leader is only loyal to school improvement and not to the principal? Who will protect the teacher leader when the teacher leader is not a member of the inner-circle and so advocates for justice despite the positioning of the principal? The teacher leader in such cases will have to find support from colleagues outside of his/her institution.

While principals need to be sensitive to teacher leaders and their actions, teacher leaders also need to be sensitive to the style of the principal and his or her approach to leadership. Both relationships must be governed by honesty, respect and mutual trust for the institution's wellbeing. Both parties must value the benefits of shared leadership underpinned by mutual respect so as to reduce power struggles and provide empowerment for learning together and learning for all.

Teacher Leadership as an Imperative

In the Jamaican context where schools face a plethora of social disparities and where many students are from resource challenged communities, teacher leaders are needed to support the work of the principal in reducing such disparities. Furthermore, teacher leadership is a necessary imperative in achieving SDG4, that of quality inclusive education for all (Ferguson, iliško, Roofe, & Hill, 2018). Teacher leaders are needed to work with principals to shift the inappropriate attitudes and maladaptive behaviours which students take with them to school. The provision of inclusive quality education requires shared leadership. Shared leadership is needed to help hold various groups accountable for their roles and for unity of purpose. Teacher leaders have a natural propensity towards mitigating issues of injustice, and so school principals need to tap into this to benefit the students, teachers and the school. Teacher leaders are influential, hence they possess power that when harnessed appropriately, can aid the achievement of school improvement goals. Their power can be utilised to influence colleagues, students and parents as well as other stakeholders outside the school. Once teacher leaders emerge in an institution, they emerge already possessing particular skill sets, hence it is for the principal to recognise these skill sets and use them to benefit the teacher leader and the institution.

I would like to add a point of caution to the readers who may only be reading this section. It is critical that one does not equate teacher leadership to being a senior teacher nor equate senior teacher to being a teacher leader. While there are senior teachers who are teacher leaders, it does not follow that because you are a senior teacher you are a teacher leader. The teacher leaders in this study emerged organically. Additionally, participants in the study were very clear that a teacher leader who is not assigned a role that appraises the teacher provides opportunities for ongoing professional development that is devoid of fear and maximises learning. Not being assigned such a role results in teachers being more open to criticism and suggestions for improvement from the teacher leader. Consequently, the construct of teacher leadership being promoted by this Jamaican study is not about a formal role of leadership, but more about the agency that resides in those who offer their expertise and those who are committed to impacting the experience of learners and their colleagues without being assigned a formal role or without knowing what the reward will be. Their sole aim is to improve the teaching and learning experience and schooling for all.

Teacher Leadership Approach is Situational

Another important insight from the findings of the study is that context matters in teacher leadership, hence there is no one-size-fits-all teacher leadership approach. Paradoxically, while the skills and competencies that teacher leaders possess can transcend context and borders, these must be utilised in light of the demands of a particular school context at a particular time. For a teacher leader to be effective, he/she must be context responsive; that is, he/she must study the problems that are unique to the particular institution and implement solutions tailored to the unique context. He/she must also know how to tailor his/her skill set to the needs of the unique context. This requires customisation in light of situational analysis in order to harness the most appropriate set of skills and competencies, thereby making the teacher leader context responsive. Consequently, a teacher leader must be an active researcher, as it is through research that he/she is able to derive evidence to support initiatives and promote the most appropriate solutions.

Maximizing the Benefits of Teacher Leadership in Jamaica

As Jamaica forges ahead to achieve quality education and VISION 2030, the following insights from this study should inform policymakers, principals and teacher preparation programmes and help to improve the landscape of teacher leadership.

Policymakers

The onus is on policymakers to ensure a clear, honest and open process of selecting school principals. This process should be one that is free from political and religious bias and one that is based on competencies appropriate to context. The National College for Educational Leadership (NCEL) and the National Education Inspectorate (NEI) established as outcomes from the recommendations from the Education Taskforce Reform of 2004 should help to aid this process—the former being responsible for training principals and the latter responsible for quality assurance and monitoring of what goes on in school.

The Ministry of Education, Youth and Information as the chief governors of schooling in Jamaica needs to demonstrate that they value shared leadership through how principals are appraised. As recommended by one of the teacher leaders in the study, feedback from teachers on how principals lead in their schools on a day-to-day basis could be incorporated during principal appraisal. This could serve to aid the principal's growth as teachers experience the principals within their local context and are best positioned to explain their strengths and areas for improvements as they together navigate the challenges of schooling within their local context.

Furthermore, the National College for Educational Leadership, through their ongoing professional development programmes, should include in their training packages a module that focuses on teacher leadership. This would provide exposure to the concept, its benefits and practicality to leaders at various levels of the education system.

Principals

With the support of their teachers, principals need to lead the development of realistic school improvement goals and utilise individual and collective agency to decide on them and achieve them. Once the goals are clearly established, communicated and agreed upon, an in-depth analysis of the human resources within the school context should be undertaken to appropriately match skill sets against school improvement goals. Since not all senior teachers are teacher leaders, while doing this the principal needs to determine the criteria used to recognise those who are teacher leaders versus those who have achieved senior teacher status so that he/she will know how to utilise the competencies to support school improvement goals. To ensure that such a process yields the intended benefits, the principal must practise honest, open communication and shared leadership to prevent injustices meted to any teacher as they exercise their individual agency. He/she must also recognise the efforts of teacher leaders and implement strategies to spot and nurture emerging teacher leaders. The principal's leadership in this sense is extremely critical since high-capacity individuals may be limited or fail to achieve agency if conditions are difficult.

Teacher Preparation Programmes in Jamaica

Considering sustainable development and the increased emphasis on student centred education in the 21st century, a cadre of teachers is needed who possess individual agency to help derive solutions to meet the needs of the whole learner. Hence, there is a need for teacher training programmes for pre-service and in-service teachers to increase emphasis on strategies, skills and concepts relating to teacher agency. Through these teachings, pre-service teacher trainees may be helped to become conscious of the innate responsibilities embedded in their roles as teachers and as members of the teaching profession. Additionally, in-service teachers may be helped to understand the social and political structures of schools and the interplay between these, their personal professional desires and what is needed to help schools improve.

Furthermore, to cultivate the sort of agency needed to benefit school improvement requires teacher educators who are agentic. Within the context of this study, an agentic teacher educator is one who is assertive, self-motivated, self-evaluative, independent in thought, yet collaborative, and is masterful at achieving goals to benefit self and others. Agentic teacher educators are needed to develop agentic teachers. If schools are to improve and benefit from systematic reform, such as those recommendations put forward by the National Education Inspectorate, a new approach to recruiting teacher educators to work in colleges of teacher training is necessary. In Jamaica, recruiting teacher educators is an autonomous activity led by the teacher training institution which is embedded in a selection process that does not always result in the most equipped or experienced teacher acquiring the job. To ensure a critical mass of critical and agentic teacher educators, a closer partnership is needed between schools and teacher training institutions, since the school is where teachers own and exhibit their practice. Additionally, a thorough analysis is needed of who these individuals are, what knowledge, skills and dispositions they need to possess to produce the quality teachers needed in Jamaica and what policy support is needed to help grow the base of teacher leaders.

References

Ferguson, T., iliško, D., Roofe, C., & Hill, S. (2018). *SDG 4 – Quality education: Inclusivity, equity and lifelong learning for all.* Bingley, United Kingdom: Emerald.

Taskforce Report (2004). Taskforce on educational reform 2004: A transformed education system. Retrieved from https://jis.gov.jm/estp/docs/Reports/JA%20 Education%20Reform%20TaskForce%20200opdf

Teacher Leadership in the United States

CHAPTER SEVEN

Teacher Leadership in the United States:

You Can't Get There from Here

ELEANOR J. BLAIR

HISTORICALLY, THE UNITED STATES has a long-standing commitment to free and public education; both the success and the failings of these schools are well-documented. Tyack and Cuban's (1995) book *Tinkering with Utopia* described the many attempts to improve and reform the work of public schools in America: "both positive and negative examples of tinkering and utopian thinking abound in the record of educational reform" (p. 1). Reforms have typically focused on three areas: teachers, curriculum, and/or the structure and organization of schools. Four questions have typically guided the organization of schools:

- What is the purpose of public schools?

- What are the roles and responsibilities of teachers? Students?

- What is the content of the curriculum?

- What is the role of democracy and advocacy for equity in public schools?

These four questions are at the heart of most heated discussions regarding the process and product of public education. And herein lies the problem:

these questions are open-ended and lend themselves to much negotiation and manipulation, but they ignore the underlying politics of public education. There are no "middle of the road" answers to these kinds of questions. Paulo Freire suggested that schools are inherently political, simultaneously operating to support the aims of one group while diminishing the needs of another group. Richard Schaull summarized this idea in the Introduction of Freire's (2000) *Pedagogy of the Oppressed*:

> There is no such thing as a neutral educational process. Education either functions as an instrument that is used to facilitate the integration of the younger generation into the logic of the present system and bring about conformity to it, *or* it becomes "the practice of freedom," the means by which men and women deal critically and creatively with reality and discover how to participate in the transformation of the world. (p. 34).

Determining the purpose of public education automatically creates a space where one group is charged with determining what kinds of knowledge must be accessed in order to achieve a set of pre-ordained purposes. Once purposes are determined, everything else follows in a linear progression. If schools are to be authoritarian and hierarchical, it only follows that teachers (and students) will be a part of that bureaucracy and carry out the tasks and responsibilities they are assigned. And of course, discussions of teacher leadership must acknowledge that the opportunities for increased power and autonomy in educational decision-making are limited by present-day politics that shape the work of educational bureaucracies. Powerful teachers do not easily "fit" into authoritarian, hierarchical institutions where power is top-down and the culture seldom reflects democratic ideals. The curriculum is similarly designed to either acquaint students with the notion that access to knowledge can be liberating or it can be prescriptive and prepare students for prescribed roles and responsibilities. It is the popular assumption of many individuals that universal access to a free and public education is a pillar of democracy; however, the reality is that access has never been equal and the fulfillment of the democratic ideals of equitable treatment within academic spaces has seldom been achieved.

Throughout history, the manipulation of variables that impact the answers to these questions have affected the lives and work of teachers and students in public school settings. And yet, schools have not changed significantly, and more importantly, teachers' work has not changed in 150 years (Cuban, 1993). Currently, dropout rates are notoriously high and the low achievement of poor children in this country are well-documented (Orfield & Lee, 2004; Howard, Banks, & Nieto, 2016). It is often difficult to remain optimistic about public schools when one considers the lack of viable, sustainable paradigm shifts that would ultimately impact public schools in meaningful ways. Teachers and teaching are most often talked about by others—politicians, educational leaders, the public—but teachers are seldom asked to participate in serious discussions of how to strengthen the professional status of teachers and access roles that provide the prerequisite power to make substantive pedagogical changes that would impact classrooms and lead to meaningful educational outcomes for both teachers and students.

The Teaching Profession and Teachers' Work

Few would dispute that the teaching profession had humble beginnings. In the mid-1800s, the opening of common schools and the expectations that all children would be provided opportunities to access a basic education were popular; however, the initial outcomes of this movement never produced equal access and the content of one's education was always shaped by race, gender, and social class. Increasingly, as attendance in common schools increased and the ideals of universal education propagated, young females were recruited to run the schools. In this way, young girls saw their educational opportunities expand. Specifically, the teaching profession simultaneously opened the doors for females acquiring higher levels of education and having jobs outside the home. Teaching became women's true profession (Hoffman, 2003). Historically, teachers have always struggled to be viewed as "real" professionals with the attributes associated with power, status, and autonomy. Teaching was often viewed in one of three ways: a job for na'er-do-wells (those who lack motivation), a job for single women (very young or very old), or an occupation for those on the way to something more meaningful; for example, doctors, lawyers, ministers, etc. The specialized skills and talents of teachers represented important, if not valued, commodities in the community, and were often treated as disposable resources lacking importance, status, or inherent value to the institution. Warren (1985) captured this idea in the following quote:

> "To call teaching a career in the nineteenth century would be mis-leading . . . for most, it was a part-time job taken up temporarily. School terms could be measured in weeks and those who taught tended to move on to other occupations or to marriage after a few years." (Finkelstein, 1970 cited in Warren, 1985, p. 6)

Fast forward to another century and it is somewhat surprising to see teachers still struggling to achieve a modicum of career status. Lortie (2002) coined the term semi-profession to describe the lack of professional status inherent to teaching, and Ingersoll (2003) noted the problems he encountered as a beginning teacher:

> Certainly, many of us who enter teaching do so knowing that it has, in most cases, never been a highly paid or highly prestigious occupation. But I was taken aback by the lack of understanding or regard for the teaching job. It seemed completely counterproduc-tive to me that many intrinsic rewards, such as the satisfaction of making an impact, or imparting one's knowledge, of working in a supportive and positive environment, and of having input into the way things operate, were lacking. (p. 3)

The circumstances of teachers' work have not changed significantly today. It is within this context that we begin an examination of teacher leadership. As discussed earlier, I believe that teacher leadership represents a road toward higher professional status, and on the other hand, I believe the attempts to recognize and support teacher leadership are doomed by those who are unwilling or unable to relinquish power and view the roles and tasks as-sociated with teaching and learning in a different manner. At times, I am even forced to consider that teacher preparation fails to prepare teachers to assume roles as teacher leaders; they are most often trained to enter public institutions where their roles are strictly defined by contractual arrangements that vary little by region or type of school. Not surprisingly, there is some degree of "push-back" at requests for teachers to consider alternative roles and responsibilities that require expanded responsibilities without additional compensation.

Attempts to negotiate changes in teachers' work lives have typically focused on three main areas: preservice teacher training at the undergraduate or graduate level; the inservice teacher experience with an emphasis on mentorship and professional development; and finally, the creation of a profession where there is mediated entry into a differentiated profession. The third focus is somewhat more complicated but offers a model for the profession that is similar to the medical profession—teachers would begin the profession as an intern or resident and at various points of documented growth and expertise, opportunities would be available to achieve higher professional status, roles, and responsibilities. The argument undergirding these efforts has been that if we want to have a better teaching profession, we have to produce a better product with more education and expertise. Simultaneously, however, would be the precondition that we have to create a different kind of context for teachers' work if we want to change the process and product of their efforts, a context that provides room for professional growth and development as well as the assumption of newly defined roles and responsibilities. Each of these approaches has the potential to be the foundation for efforts to produce better teachers working in healthier work environments that support the growth of teacher leadership. And yet, at this time, none of these efforts have produced lasting changes in the lives and work of teachers, and if anything, teaching seems to be moving backward rather than forward; for example, some states have removed incentives for advanced degrees among teachers, and the increased focus on accountability has shifted much of the focus in schools to student achievement rather than teacher professionalism, mentorship, and professional growth and development. While the 20th century was transformed by industrialization, urbanization, and immigration, the 21st century seemed to offer a similar set of change agents in the shape of technology, globalization, and diversity. The world is changing in ways that make us more connected within a context that requires digital literacy and even higher standards of excellence, and yet, rather than embracing change, we seem to be stumbling and looking backwards for answers to the future. George and Louise Spindler (1982) argued that we need to "make the familiar strange and strange familiar" in our thinking about schools. In this way, we have the opportunity to recognize the lack of fit between many of our school practices and current demographics, and perhaps, consider new and different "solutions" that require us to disrupt the current narrative of public education and reconsider our answers to the four questions posed at the beginning of this chapter.

Albert Einstein (n.d.) once said, "If I had an hour to solve a problem I'd spend 55 minutes thinking about the problem and 5 minutes thinking about solutions." The point, I believe, is found in another quote, "How you define the problem determines the solution." Too often we spend more time on the solution than on thinking deeply about the different layers of the problem. Few problems are simple, but in our quest to come up with quick and simple solutions, we ignore complex, hard-to-solve problems and look for the simple issue. For example, look at low test scores. We can fix test scores by simply doing a better job of teaching the test. Far more difficult is an analysis of low test scores that reveals that poverty, homelessness, domestic violence, neglect, and/or addiction issues contribute to the inability of a child to focus and learn successfully. Those kinds of problems are societal issues that require multi-agency solutions. Policy makers—educators and/or politicians—recognize that it is easier to just focus on test scores and ignore the larger issues that impact teaching and learning in profound ways. As such, one of the problems encountered when talking about teacher leadership and the status of the teaching profession is understanding how we got to this place and why the teaching profession has been stubbornly resistant to real change. Teachers' voices are seldom a part of school reform discussions; rather, they are talked *about* as if they were not key subjects in the discussion, but rather benign, and perhaps at times annoying, bystanders. In this way, fixing problems in education only requires us to tell teachers what they are doing wrong and how they will now fix it; teachers are a part of the problem only when they resist this process and insist on becoming the "public face" of schools and acting autonomously. In most current hierarchical models of educational bureaucracies, there is no room for teacher leadership; teachers are simply a part of the process of achieving previously defined quotas and test data that support educational objectives and provide a foundation for the solicitation of financial resources. Could it be that the "real" issues driving national discussions about public schools have little to do with teachers' work and more to do with national concerns that are guided by corporate models that attempt to define school success in economic terms? If so, it is easier to understand how a focus on narrow (and behavioral) definitions of success that utilize strict models of accountability and rely entirely on standardized test data have taken over the national conversation on school success. This kind of focus on strict accountability and measurable outcomes even extends into teacher preparation and licensure; e.g., the Pearson tests. Pearson textbooks and tests for licensure and entry into the teaching profession have become the norm in many colleges of education as well as public schools, with few challenges to the premises undergirding their materials. Questions and/or debate and discussion about the Pearson model and its ideological roots have been sidelined. And yet, the Pearson corporation grows unchecked; their wealth and influence are seldom questioned by policymakers, or more importantly, by faculty and students impacted by the imposition of homogeneous corporate models of good teaching and learning. The loss of voice—consenting and/or dissenting—in these discussion is a part of the problem; if we don't spend the prerequisite time understanding the problem, the solutions will always be flawed. York-Barr and Duke (2004) discuss the impact of school culture on teacher leadership and the impact of "long-standing norms of the teaching profession" challenging the prospects of teacher leadership (p. 270). They argue that "teachers have been socialized to be private, to be followers, and to steer away from assuming responsibilities outside of the classroom" (p. 270). A powerful obstacle to teacher leadership is the tendency within the profession for egalitarianism; e.g., teacher leaders may be perceived as "stepping out of line" or assuming roles that grant too much power and authority to a teacher (p. 272). In this way, teacher leaders in both formal and informal roles may be victims of what Duke (1994) referred to as the "crab bucket mentality" (cited in York-Barr & Duke, 2004, p. 272). He explained that, "when one is crabbing, no lid is required to keep the crabs in the bucket because crabs will reach up and drag each other down should one attempt to climb out." In this way, the school culture "strangles" attempts to nurture and sustain teacher leadership. The emergence of "new" school cultures that support teachers as learners and leaders in schools that value professional learning communities and share accountability for professional development and overall school outcomes are necessary for teacher leadership to thrive. However, in the spirit of having broad-based participation by teachers in school-based reform efforts, teachers must take the initiative to build and support alternatives to the status quo, and more importantly begin the process of reflecting on the school culture and current practices that undermine the efforts of teacher leaders.

Teaching: A Profession in Crisis

Other signs that teaching as a profession is in trouble continue to emerge in the educational landscape. A decline in enrollment in teacher education programs and high levels of attrition in the profession seem to indicate that teaching is becoming a profession of "last resort." A recent *Education Week* story (March 17, 2019) provided the following data:

> Between the 2007-08 and 2015-16 academic years, there was a 23 percent decline in the number of people completing teacher-preparation programs. The largest decline—32 percent—has been at alternative programs (for people who already have a bachelor's degree) that are housed in colleges or universities. But all types of programs have seen drops...The number of bachelor's degrees conferred in education declined by 15 percent between 2005-06 and 2014-15. ("Enrollment is down at teachers' colleges, so they're to change," 2018, n.p.)

Individuals entering teaching are typically full of hope and ambition, and yet, too often, they leave within five years and take their dreams elsewhere. Recently, Ravitch (2010) noted:

> Between 40 percent and 50 percent of new teachers do not survive the first five years. Maybe they couldn't manage the classes; maybe they were disappointed by working conditions; maybe teaching was not for them; maybe they felt that they were unsuccessful; or maybe they decided to enter another profession. For whatever reason, the job is so demanding that nearly half of those who enter teaching choose to leave at an early stage in their career. (p. 177)

Recent data from the Learning Policy Institute confirms the emergence of problems associated with teacher turnover:

> When students return to school this year, many will enter one of the more than 100,000 classrooms across the country staffed by an instructor who is not fully qualified to teach. This is because many districts, facing ongoing teacher shortages, are hiring under-qualified candidates to fill vacancies. While shortages tend to draw attention to recruitment issues, this report finds that 90% of open teaching positions are created by teachers who leave the profession. Some are retiring, but about 2/3 of teachers leave for other reasons, most due to dissatisfactions with teaching. Teacher attrition in the United States is about twice as high as in high-achieving jurisdictions like Finland, Singapore, and Ontario, Canada. (Carver-Thomas & Darling-Hammond, 2017, n.p.)

Teacher attrition seriously impedes efforts to positively impact the teaching profession. Among teachers who are dissatisfied with their positions, Phillips (2015) found that, "over the next five years....nearly half of those teachers will transfer to a new school or leave the profession altogether — only to be replaced with similarly fresh-faced teachers" (para. 2). Phillips' interview of Richard Ingersoll provides insights from Ingersoll's research on teacher turnover and retention, "One of the reasons teachers quit, he says, is that they feel they have no say in decisions that ultimately affect their teaching" (para. 5). Ingersoll acknowledges that salary is an issue, but not the main issue. He argues that there are larger issues that impact teacher attrition: "One of the main factors is the issue of voice, and having say, and being able to have input into the key decisions in the building that affect a teacher's job. This is something that is a hallmark of professions. It's something that teachers usually have very little of, but it does vary across schools and it's very highly correlated with the decision whether to stay or leave" (para. 9). Teachers today are better educated than ever before in our history. A recent article in NEA Today provided the following insights on teacher education:

> The percentage of public school teachers who hold a post baccalaureate degree (i.e., a master's, education specialist, or doctoral de-

gree) has increased since 1999-2000. Fifty-seven percent had such a degree in 2016, compared to 47 percent in 2000. This trend is evident at both the elementary and secondary levels. Roughly 55 percent of elementary school teachers and 59 percent of secondary school teachers held a post baccalaureate degree in 2015–16, whereas 45 and 50 percent, respectively, held a post baccalaureate degree in 1999–2000. (Walker, 2018, n.p.)

These teachers have earned the right to have a voice and a say in important decision-making matters; "a place at the table" is the next step for professional growth and development and reflects a recognition of professional status and respect. And yet, there are numerous reasons why teachers have not been able to advance the profession toward higher professional status. One of the easiest explanations has to do with gender, sexism, and the allocation of power and resources. Teaching has long been considered women's work. Yes, there are men in education, but they are a minority and many of the men who enter teaching quickly advance to administrative roles. "According to the Consortium for Policy Research in Education, only about 24 percent of all teachers were male in 2012, with just one in 10 men teaching elementary school students" (Deese, 2017, para. 5). And yet, while teachers dominate the classroom, educational administrators, who make higher salaries and have greater power over the schools, are primarily male. Recent data in an *Education Week* essay documented a decidedly male influence in the running of American schools:

Even though K-12 education is largely a female enterprise, men dominate the chief executive's office in the nation's nearly 14,000 districts, numbers that look especially bleak given that the pool of talent is deep with women. Women make up 76 percent of teachers, 52 percent of principals, and 78 percent of central-office administrators, according to federal data and the results of a recent national survey. Yet they account for less than a quarter of all superintendents, according to a survey conducted this summer by AASA, the School Superintendents Association. (Superville, 2017, para. 5)

Viewed overwhelmingly as a woman's profession, teaching may be associated with antiquated views of women's roles; women may not be seen as heads of households or primary breadwinners. More impactful may be views that women should not be in positions of power and authority. Perhaps women are not viewed as being fit to be leaders. The teaching profession has suffered numerous setbacks over the past decade, and not surprisingly, teachers are increasingly seeking ways to make their voices heard despite continuing efforts to ignore their requests to be recognized, rewarded, and included in important decision-making that impacts their lives and work. It does not seem like a stretch to propose that the status of women in American society may be reflected in the way that we view teachers. It is not surprising to me that in this historic moment of the #MeToo movement in America that we simultaneously see unprecedented numbers of teachers, female as well as male, taking to the streets to demand that their voices be heard, to declare that they will not be silenced anymore. The intersection of power and gender in the teaching profession presents challenges to notions of teacher leadership and its relationship to the advancement of the larger profession of teachers. Individuals in powerful positions are often the greatest foes in this effort to achieve more power and autonomy for teachers. Efforts to redefine the roles of teachers and seek equitable relationships between teachers and the mostly male educational administrators is fraught with uncertainty, uneasiness, and at times, outright anger and resistance. Many people will talk about equity and equal rights among men and women, but "on the ground" and in the face of current realities, the relinquishment or sharing of power and authority is easier talked about than done.

Twenty-first Century School Issues: The Big Picture

Compliance and silence today is more dangerous than ever for teachers, and more importantly, for our children. Twenty-first century schools are daily confronted with the evidence of their failures as they see increasingly large numbers of poor children coming from ethnically and racially diverse backgrounds not finding success in the public schools (Aud, Fox, & KewalRamani, 2010). A key piece of the transformation and re-visioning of teachers' work is the role of advocacy for children who are *falling through the cracks* in our schools. Perhaps, the more serious questions for teacher educators relate to strategies for producing teacher leaders who are both critical ped-agogues and advocacy leaders. Giroux's (1988) words still seem applicable:

> The political and ideological climate does not look favorable for teachers at the moment. But it does offer them the challenge to join in a public debate with their critics as well as the opportunity to engage in a much-needed self-critique regarding the nature and purpose of teacher preparation, in-service teacher programs and the dominant forms of classroom teaching. Similarly, the debate provides teachers with the opportunity to organize collectively to improve the conditions under which they work and to demonstrate to the public the central role that teachers must play in any viable attempt to reform the public schools. (p. 122)

The profession needs teacher leaders, schools need teacher leaders, but most importantly, our children need teacher leaders. Teacher leaders are on the front-line of the work we are doing in schools, and as such, teachers must be in roles where they are decision-makers, not merely implementers of policies and procedures handed down to them. In this way, school improvement can occur spontaneously and children benefit from being a part of classrooms where assessment, diagnosis, and remediation of pedagogical issues is a fluid process led by teachers. Teachers today are better educated than ever before in the history of the United States. Teachers, as a group, are thoughtful and reflective about teaching practices. Not only do teachers know how to teach, they simultaneously know how to be both consumers and producers of research that is relevant to their classrooms and students. Teachers are the primary advocates for students, and as such, the advocacy leadership that Anderson (2009) promotes is a key piece of teacher leadership that is transformative.

Add to this scenario recent news coverage documenting the high lev-els of teacher moonlighting, teachers who work second jobs and/or seek other sources of income just to survive financially, and you have a recipe for a professional disaster (Blair, 2018). The Greek philosopher, Heraclitus, wisely said that change is the only constant we face, however; resistance to change is the greatest challenge to new definitions of teachers' work. So much is wrong with the profession that there are days when talking about teacher leadership seems like a futile cause. However, for all of the things that are wrong with the profession, there is so much that is right. Teachers make a difference in the lives of children and in the future of the country, and as such, making the profession stronger and better is a noble cause— an important cause. As I began this book with at a vision of what teacher leadership could mean to the profession, I was forced to simultaneously recognize that meaningful change will only occur when the debate over power and leadership and the role of teachers expands and moves beyond the cyclical arguments and complaints that have defined teachers' work for so many decades. Educational settings must be re-formed and re-visioned in new images and previous narratives, by necessity, must be expanded to include roles that are defined by equitable communication, collaboration, and decision-making. Hence the quote attributed to Malcolm X: "We can't teach what we don't know, and we can't lead where we won't go." If teacher leaders want to begin to do work that promotes a higher professional status for teachers and honors social justice and advocacy as integral parts of teacher leadership, they must be willing to make the challenging, and often difficult journey into uncharted territory.

References

Anderson, G. (2009). *Advocacy leadership: Toward a post-reform agenda in education*. New York: Routledge.

Aud, S, Fox, M., & KewalRamani, A. (2010). *Status and trends in the education of racial and ethnic groups*. U.S. Department of Education, Institute of Education Sciences, and National Center for Education Statistics.

Blair, E. (2018). *By the light of the silvery moon: Teacher moonlighting and the dark side of teachers' work*. Gorham, ME: Myers Education Press.

Carver-Thomas, D., & Darling-Hammond, L. (2017, August 16). Teacher turnover: Why it matters and what we can do about it. Learning Policy Institute. Retrieved from https://learningpolicyinstitute.org/product/teacher-turnover-report

Cuban, L. (1993) (2nd Edition). *How teachers taught: Constancy and change in American classrooms 1890-1990*. New York: Teachers College Press.

Deese, H. (2017, July 22). Male teacher shortage affects boys who need male role models. *USA Today*. Retrieved from https://www.usatoday.com/story/news/2017/07/22/male-teacher-shortage-affects-boys-who-need-role-models/103585138/

Duke, D.L. (1994). Drift, detachment, and the need for teacher leadership. In D.R. Walling (Ed.), *Teachers as leaders: Perspectives on the professional development of leaders*, (pp. 225–273). Bloomington, IN: Phi Delta Kappan Educational Foundation.

Enrollment is down at teachers' colleges, so they're to change. (2019, March 19). *Education Week*. Retrieved from https://www.edweek.org/ew/articles/2018/08/09/enrollment-is-down-at-teacher-colleges-so.html

Einstein, A. (n.d.). Retrieved from https://medium.com/an-idea-for-you/how-well-you-define-a-problem-determines-how-well-you-solve-it-847090979898

Finkelstein, B. J. (1970). *Governing the young: Teacher behavior in American primary schools, 1820–1880*. Unpublished doctoral dissertation, Teachers College, Columbia University.

Freire, P. (2000). *Pedagogy of the oppressed* (30th Anniversary Edition). New York: Continuum.

Giroux, H. (1988). *Teachers as intellectuals: Toward a critical pedagogy of learning*. Westport, Ct: Bergin & Garvey.

Hoffman, N. (2003). *Women's true profession: Voices from the history of teaching* (2nd ed.). Cambridge, MA: Harvard Education Press.

Howard, G., Banks, J., & Nieto, S. (2016). *We can't teach what we don't know: White teachers, multiracial schools* (3rd ed.). New York: Teachers College Press.

Ingersoll, R.M. (2003). *Who controls teachers' work: Power and accountability in teachers' work*. Cambridge, MA: Harvard Education Press.

Lortie, D. (2002). *Schoolteacher* (2nd ed.). Chicago: University of Chicago Press.

Orfield, G. & Lee, C. (2004). *Why segregation matters: Poverty and education inequality*. Cambridge, MA: The Civil Rights Project, Harvard University. Retrieved from https://civilrightsproject.ucla.edu/research/k-12-education/integration-and-diversity/why-segregation-matters-poverty-and-educational-inequality/orfield-why-segregation-matters-2005.pdf

Phillips, O. (2015). Revolving door of teachers costs schools billions every year. nprED: How learning happens. Retrieved from https://www.npr.org/sections/ed/2015/03/30/395322012/the-hidden-costs-of-teacher-turnover

Ravitch, D. (2010). *The death and life of the great American school system: How testing and choice are undermining education*. New York: Basic Books.

Spindler, G., & Spindler, L. (1982). Roger Harker and Schöenhausen: From familiar to strange and back again. In G. Spindler (Ed.), *Doing the ethnography of schooling: Educational anthropology in action* (pp. 20–46). New York, NY: Holt, Rinehart, and Winston.

Superville, D. (2017, March 8). Few women run the nation's school districts. Why? *Education Week*. Retrieved from https://www.edweek.org/ew/articles/2016/11/16/few-women-run-the-nations-school-districts.html

Tyack, D., & Cuban, L. (1995). *Tinkering toward utopia*. Boston, MA: Harvard University Press.

Walker, T. (2018). Who is the average U.S. teacher. *NEA Today*. Retrieved from http://neatoday.org/2018/06/08/who-is-the-average-u-s-teacher/

Warren, D. (1985). *Learning from experience: History and teacher education*. Educational Researcher, 14(10), 5–12.

York-Barr, J., & Duke, K. (2004, Autumn). What do we know about teacher leadership? Findings from two decades of scholarship. *Review of Educational Research, 74*(3), 255–316.

CHAPTER EIGHT

Teacher Leaders Today:

Teachers Talk About Their Work

Eleanor J. Blair

In North Carolina, all teachers are expected to be leaders. The North Carolina State Board of Education charged the North Carolina Professional Teaching Standards Commission to align the Core Standards for the Teaching Profession in 1997 (North Carolina Professional Teaching Standards, 2013) with this vision in mind. Commission members, 16 practicing educators from across the state, considered what teachers need to know and be able to do in 21st-century schools (North Carolina Professional Teaching Standards, 2008, p. 1). The six standards were aligned and adopted by the North Carolina State Board of Education in June 2007 and July 2011. "The North Carolina Professional Teaching Standards are the basis for teacher preparation, teacher evaluation, and professional development. Each of these will include the skills and knowledge needed for the 21st century teaching and learning" (North Carolina Professional Teaching Standards, 2008, p. 1). Only one of the six standards addresses teacher leadership; the other standards address pedagogical knowledge, reflection, and the needs of students. In Standard One, "Teachers Demonstrate Leadership," the following teacher behaviors are included:

- Teachers lead in their classrooms.
  - Teachers demonstrate leadership by taking responsibility for the progress of all students to ensure that they graduate from high school, are globally competitive for work and postsecondary education, and are prepared for life in the 21st century.

- Teachers demonstrate leadership in the school.
  - Teachers work collaboratively with school personnel to create a professional learning community. They analyze and use local, state, and national data to develop goals and strategies in the school improvement plan that enhances student learning and teacher working conditions.

- Teachers lead the teaching profession.
  - Teachers strive to improve the teaching profession. They contribute to the establishment of positive working conditions in their school. They actively participate in and advocate for decision-making structures in education and government that take advantage of the expertise of teachers.

- Teachers advocate for schools and students.
  - Teachers advocate for positive change in policies and practices affecting student learning. They participate in the implementation of initiatives to improve the education of students.

- Teachers demonstrate high ethical standards.
  - Teachers demonstrate ethical principles including honesty, integrity, fair treatment, and respect for others. Teachers uphold the Code of Ethics for North Carolina Educators (effective June 1, 1997) and the Standards for Professional Conduct adopted April 1, 1998. (North Carolina Professional Teaching Standards, 2008, p. 2)

Taken as a sub-group of a larger vision, Standard One, nevertheless, provides a roadmap for meaningful and sustainable teacher leadership in North Carolina schools. The deprivatization of teachers' work in combination with collaborative efforts to create professional learning communities that foster pedagogical practices that are supported by research and scholarship will have the potential to impact the culture of teachers' work. However, changing the culture of schools is not an easy task and the "mapping" of this work must be accompanied by explicit directions for how teacher leaders are able to survive (and thrive) within traditional hierarchical bureaucracies. It is important to note that within Standard One, the first three behaviors explicitly involve leadership, but there is an acknowledgement of the significant roles of advocacy and ethics as important aspects of emergent teacher leadership—qualities that match up nicely with the Center for Strengthening the Teaching Profession (CSTP) *Teacher Leadership Skills Framework* that highlights the role of trust, integrity, and equity in teacher leadership. The North Carolina Professional Teaching Standards are intended to guide teacher preparation, and as such Standard One provides a foundation for the work that I do in my teacher leadership classes. However, seldom discussed is the issue that while these standards do represent a provocative vision for teachers' work, they are not supported by resources that are prerequisite for the training and development that would support the work of teachers and principals trying to negotiate and navigate a new and expanded vision for teacher leadership.

Within this context, the study of North Carolina teacher leaders seemed timely and appropriate. Twelve teachers participated in the research project. I selected currently practicing teachers who are in enrolled in graduate education programs of study. One of the teachers was currently a practicing teacher who had been recognized for her leadership skills through regional awards and/or promotion to formal leadership positions; e.g., instructional coach. Most were working on either a Master of Arts in Teaching (MAT) or a Master's in Education (MAED) degree. These teachers represented a wide sampling of teachers with regard to age and experiences, but the information they provided was remarkably consistent across groups.

Each of the teachers responded to the questions from the interview protocol and these responses were later subjected to a phenomenological analysis where common themes and categories of information were identified. The purpose of the data reduction and analysis was to describe the personal meanings that each of the teachers attributed to their work as teachers and as leaders. Themes and categories of themes emerged from this analysis that seem to describe the structure of individual understandings regarding teachers' work. Colaizzi's (1978) work in this area still captures the basic process that was undertaken:

1. "Making sense" of the original protocol,

2. Extracting significant statements,

3. Formulating meanings,

4. Organizing the aggregate formulated meanings into clusters of themes,

5. Referring the clusters of themes back to the original protocols in order to validate them,

6. Formulating an exhaustive description of the investigated phenomenon. (p. 59)

Table 8.1: Teacher Demographics

Teacher	Gender	Race/ Ethnicity	Experience	Job	Education	Age
#EM	F	White	11 years	Science, Technology, Engineering and Math (STEM)/Elementary	BS/MAT	56
#DK	F	White	5 years	Special Education (K-12)	BS/LATERAL ENTRY	40
#LP	F	White	4 years	Special Education (K-12)	BS/MAED	29
#NB	F	African American	2 years	Special Education (Middle School)	BS/MAT	30
#KR	F	White	3 years	Special Education/ English as a Second Language (ESL)/Art Elementary	BS/MAT	26
#SS	F	White	16 years	High School	BS/MAED/ MSA/MAT	40
#VM	F	White	1 year	Special Education (K-12)	BA/MAT	31
#TG	M	Latino/ Hispanic	2 years	Kindergarten/ English as a Second Language (ESL)	BS/MAT	24
#OH	F	White	8 years	Instructional Coach	BS/MAT	29
#HP	F	White	6 years	Middle and High School/Special Educational	BS/MAT	29
#KJ	F	African American	2 years	Special Education	BS/MAT	32
#TM	F	White	6 years	Special Education/ Middle School	BS/MAT	45

Following a process similar to the one used by Acker-Hocevar and Touch-ton (1999), I took the following steps: (1) identified the units of information in typed transcripts, (2) established several working categories to locate the specific units, (3) grouped the categories together to identify major subthemes across all the interviews, and (4) combined subthemes into five major themes. The themes were: (1) Career dilemmas: Becoming a teacher, (2) School culture: We are family, (3) Flavors of teacher leadership, (4) The Complexities of power and decision-making: Teacher leadership as an island, and (5) Personal power, advocacy, and social justice: What's love got to do with it? Accurately conveying what each of the teachers said in the interviews is an important component of this study. Thus, whenever possible, I have used the actual words of the individual teachers. In this way, readers of this research may see other themes or dimensions in the study that did not appear in my analysis. The preliminary analysis included checks with the teachers to ensure that the intent of their words and my descriptions were consistent.

1. Career Dilemmas: Becoming a Teacher

The road to becoming a teacher was full of surprises for most of the teachers who participated in this study. While we often think of the traditional road to the classroom as consisting of college, an education major, graduation, and first teaching job in one's early 20s, this was not the case in many of the stories I was told by the interviewees. For several of the interviewees, teaching became a career option after they had graduated with other majors in other areas:

> After being unable to find anything in technical writing right out of college, I decided to use my English degree to try teaching English to 7th graders. I ended up really disliking it because I was unable to do anything other than teach to a test rather than access them in other ways like projects and presentations. (#KR)

> I joke that I became a teacher by accident because my parents insisted I apply for a scholarship in high school and Teaching Fellows is what was available at the time. I made it to the regional round

but did not receive the scholarship; however, I continued to pursue education. (#SS)

My undergraduate degree is in psychology. I decided that I would like to work with exceptional needs children after spending the summer as a respite care provider for a five-year-old on the severe end of the autism spectrum. (#VM)

I would graduate in 2015 with a major in studio art and Spanish. Three months later I accepted the position of artist in residence at The Bascom: A Center for the Visual Arts where I stayed for nearly two years. (#TG)

Prior to becoming an educator, I worked in the corporate world (middle management) for almost twenty years . . . My journey to the classroom and to teaching was not what I had planned. I left my corporate position to spend time with my children. (#EM)

I began my coursework in the area of communication disorders, but graduated with a degree in recreational therapy. I have always had desire to help others . . . I was presented with the opportunity to also help children in the school system by being an applied behavior analysis instructor assistant . . . As I grew in this position and gained a wealth of hands on experience, I was presented the opportunity to become a classroom teacher for this population. (#DK)

However, for others, there was always an interest in working with children, but the exact population of students that would become their "calling" did not become evident until other experiences intervened.

I originally went to school to become an elementary teacher and went through with the degree. However, I did not find a job like I thought I would and started substituting at the school I ended up getting a job at. I fell in love with special needs students while subbing and decided to get my add-on license in special education. (#LP)

I always wanted to work with children but I was not sure to what capacity. It wasn't until I started working with a teen volunteer who had autism that I knew I wanted to work with children with disabilities. (#NB)

Considering these circumstances as a backdrop to any discussion of teacher leadership brings up previously unexplored considerations. If one never intended to be a teacher, one may not have given a lot of thought to the realities of teaching. I have often observed that individuals choose to teach for one of two reasons; first, they hated school and had miserable experiences and they want to do a "re-do" and help other students who also hate school; or second, they enjoyed school, but never thought about teaching until an interaction with a child or a group of students caused them to think about it differently. Of course, there is a third reason, one that causes some additional concerns; some people simply can't find a job and teaching seems like a viable alternative. For any of these aforementioned reasons, individuals may be drawn to teaching, but perhaps, due to a lack of understanding about the challenges of teaching—the low salary, difficult working conditions, and lack of status and recognition—these same teachers may quickly leave the profession when they discover that helping a child or making a difference is simply not enough to make teaching one's life work. This may explain the high rates of attrition and mobility among teachers. What is hard to ascertain is whether these issues are unique to teaching. Do more people assume *apriori* that they know something about teaching simply because they have been students or parents of students for a large part of their lives? Teaching is unique in that almost everyone has prior knowledge about schools, but this knowledge is deceptive; being a student is quite different from being a teacher. Additionally, teaching is situational; teaching in a white, suburban, or rural school is quite different from teaching in an increasingly diverse urban area.

Teaching is hard work, and yes, it can be rewarding and gratifying, but the selection of a profession that one wants to commit a life to requires a broader commitment to more than just a child or a classroom. Work in education is political and ideological. Discussions of agency and power within a leadership context are difficult when there has been little preparation for an advocacy role. Working in a teacher leadership role includes work that is shaped by politics and ideology, plus a desire to lead, direct, and facilitate; none of this is regularly included in pre-service teacher preparation. In this way, "becoming a teacher" is a complicated process of growth and development that begins on day one and continues throughout one's career. Under the best circumstances, this process is nurtured and supported by mentors, but under the worst circumstances, it contributes to early teacher attrition.

2. School Culture: We are Family

School culture is often cited by teachers as an important dimension of their work. When I visit schools that have leaders who are described as distant, punitive, and authoritarian, I find teachers who describe themselves as "deflated." Accompanying this deflation are feelings of anger and distrust—distrust among teachers as well as between teachers and administrators. I like to say that I can detect an aura when I enter a school; it is either upbeat and positive or it feels like a "black hole" of negativity. I am not always 100 percent correct; there are variations on every theme, but negative schools leave me with an uneasiness and a desire to quickly leave. For obvious reasons, teacher leaders have few choices in schools that reflect a top-down model of leadership that leaves teachers in powerless positions where survival becomes a major goal and the needs of children take a back seat to the needs of adults. These schools are often chaotic environments where there is no vision, no clearly defined curriculum, no professional development, low achievement, and rampant school discipline problems. Teachers want to leave, not lead.

However, in more positive contexts, teachers regularly discussed the importance of collaboration and communication in the schools where they worked. These schools may not be perfect; there may be inherent flaws in the leadership and collegiality that exist in the school, but more often than not, there is a vision of the schoolhouse as a family-type environment where each system works in concert with the other parts of the educational program. Words like "supportive," "positive," "respect," and "cooperative" were used to describe these work environments. There was a feeling of positive energy and an overarching belief that through working together, they could make a difference.

> One word, family . . . I am able to approach administration as easily as I can another assistant teacher . . . the cohesiveness of the staff provides a positive, nurturing learning environment where the students are able to learn and grow as individuals. . . . The school culture is generally very positive and not very stressful. There is a respect of all staff, from administration to staff and staff to administration. (#EM)

> I have been blessed with strong mentors and encouraging support throughout my career so that even when I did not see the leader in me, someone else did and encouraged me along. I found that I thoroughly enjoyed working with adults a much as I did students. (#SS)

> The school culture where I work can probably be best described as diverse. Our special education department is extremely supportive, positive, and cooperative, which makes coming to work each day even better. There are other teachers in the building who are not that way unfortunately. I would say that those are who make the job more difficult, but I like to stay away from the negativity or those who are constantly complaining. (#TM)

> When the expectations and instructional focus is unclear, please flounder . . . More than anything else, people support teachers' work. When you work with a dynamic group of educators who truly care about students' best interests and a leader who is clear on expectations and the instructional focus, anything can be achieved. You can deal with a lack of resources and diverse needs when you have a supportive team. However, when you feel alone, the task feels unbearable. (#OH)

> Looking at the school culture from last year, I can definitely say that the teachers as a whole seem to mesh really well, we're supportive,

and it feels like we actually are a family. We are providing support to each other and working collaboratively to make sure that the needs of our students are being met. (#NB)

I feel like our school is for the most part, a family (we call ourselves the NAMily). (#LP)

At our school, team leaders are often involved with conversation with the administration team. . . . Teachers, for the most part, appear to be okay with the relationships because they may realize that these relationships may sometimes include additional work or responsibility. (#EM)

My first school forced all my planning time into meeting with my mentor and PLC. I was unable to have time for me to actually create worksheets and grade, so I would spend all my time at home doing things for school. The professional development I was forced to do for first year teachers was terrible. I was told to do one thing then told by another person to do another. It was so confusing. (#KR)

However, teachers also discussed the impact of co-workers who were negative and prone to frequent complaining or simply the lack of organization and structure to support new teachers. Chasms within the school culture were evident in the tensions that arose between grades, content areas, and even between administrators and teachers.

Everyone is into themselves. There is a lot of politics. Some teachers are good buddies with each other and they only support their buddies. . . . Being a beginning teacher, I feel there is no support. You are basically all alone and have to reach out for help. (#KJ)

First, it is difficult to work with unclear leaders. When the expectations and instructional focus is unclear, people flounder. (#OH)

There seems to be a lot of friction at times and a lot of gossiping and complaining behind doors. I barely know some of the teachers and there is little sense of community in the school. (#TG)

Several of the teachers who participated in the study discussed the Leader in Me School Program that follows the seven habits designed and written by Stephen Covey (2013). The program seems to promote positive, democratic school environments and received favorable reviews from teachers:

We have both a teacher lighthouse team and a student lighthouse team. These teams are designed to lead and guide instruction, activities, and the culture of the school environment. Our principal is a democratic leader who works with both the student lighthouse and the teacher lighthouse teams to design an environment where students can grow and develop their own unique leadership style. (#HP)

Hargreaves (1994) identifies five broad forms of teacher culture: individualism, collaboration, contrived collegiality, balkanization, and the moving mosaic. He posits that the success or failure of educational change can be attributed to these different forms (relationships) of teacher culture in the school (cited in Acker-Hocevar and Touchton, 1999, p. 12). Clearly, school culture cannot be ignored in efforts to establish higher levels of teacher leadership in a school, and yet, principals and teachers will often either ignore or trivialize efforts to build a more positive school culture.

Difficult questions have to be answered as a prerequisite to understanding school culture. It is important to seriously analyze the legitimacy of efforts to collaborate, communicate, and bring people together to share power and decision-making. Within any context, questions have to be asked regarding the "hoarding" of power as well as the lack of enthusiasm one might find among individuals who are reluctant to assume additional responsibilities and relationships that expand one's professional roles and responsibilities. A preliminary annual activity of any school should be the discussion and framing of a school vision (a journey) that determines current status (a beginning) as well as end goals and objectives (and ending). The roles and responsibilities of both teachers and administrators that are required to achieve these goals and measure both success and failure is an intimate part of this activity. In this way, school culture becomes a complicated part of the discussion about teacher leadership. The teachers in this study reflect many different viewpoints, but they never failed to emphasize the impact that the culture of the school had on their efforts to be leaders. And yet, none of the teachers interviewed for this study discussed ongoing efforts to supplement, enhance, or even recognize the importance of a dynamic school culture and/or the need for regular attempts to re-vision and address changes within the infrastructure and the larger community of major stakeholders.

3. Flavors of Teacher Expertise

Most considerations of teacher leadership acknowledge the role of teacher knowledge and expertise. Interviews with teachers revealed many different views of teacher expertise. Philip Schlechty (1993) discusses the five types of roles that may be assumed by teacher leaders doing the work of restructuring and embracing change in schools—trailblazers, pioneers, settlers, stay-at-homes, and saboteurs: "Those who play these roles have vastly different training and support needs" (p. 47). Additionally, each of these roles has different motives that drive their work as teacher leaders. As such, "to create commitment, one must understand motives" (p. 50). Understanding the motives and the types of expertise that is reflected in each of these roles is a reflection of the different "flavors" that are reflected in teacher leadership work. For most, teacher expertise was specialized knowledge and content; however, others could not talk about expertise without discussing the intersection of mentorship and collaboration with teacher knowledge. For example,

> I would define teacher expertise as having knowledge that "something special" that teachers put into their classroom. It is also simply being a good educator. As a beginning teacher, I observed many other teachers and saw many flavors of teacher expertise. (#KR)

Teacher expertise in my opinion is when you have full knowledge of not only your content area but also knowing how to use this knowledge to help improve your entire school. I've found that depending on the teacher and their relationship with members of administration, they are able to use their knowledge and expertise more confidently. . . . Once I became a teacher leader and gained the respect of my team and administration, I continue to use my expertise that allows me to be involved with decision-making that affects my program. (#NB)

I always support others in whatever they decide to do. I'm more of the behind-the-scenes type of person. (#KJ)

Teacher expertise is their knowledge of the content they teach . . . this expertise does lend to your thoughts and opinions being heard, especially if it pertains to your area. (#LP)

Teacher expertise is not only about knowing your content, but about being able to connect it and being able to readily share with other teachers in the school, the district, or beyond. All teachers have expertise in something that can be shared in order to make our school a better place. (#EM)

I do not have the full knowledge and experience that lead to the credentials, but I do have that end goal in mind. I am building my skill set to help not only myself in my career goals, but to be a better educator to my students and well-informed resource to other teachers. . . . Teachers are as involved as they want to be. For some their role in the school is not just a career choice, but a large part of their daily life due to the many roles that they chose to partake of within the school. (#VM)

I would define teacher expertise as having the ability and tools to handle teaching, and knowing when and why to employ each tool. . . . Teachers who have a high level of expertise are often put in leadership roles or are asked to serve as mentors for beginning teachers. Because of this, having core expertise allows you the opportunity to be more involved in the decision-making teams in the school. (#OH)

Because of his lack of experience, he frequently seeks advice from a lead teacher to construct lesson plans. He allows me to teach social skills or take over lessons when he has meetings in order to support my development in teaching. While he is not experienced, he is frequently able to find the right person to ask when I have questions. (#VM)

Teacher expertise in my opinion is a complex definition. It is not as simple as years of experience or obtaining excellent ratings on observations; it goes beyond that and dives into student relationships, differentiation, accommodations, and cooperation with colleagues. (#TM)

Understanding how teachers acknowledge and use expertise is an important dimension of teacher leadership. The Center for Strengthening the Teaching Profession (CSTP) (2018) provides a framework of skills necessary for teacher leadership. In their definition of teacher leadership, the emphasis is on the role of expertise. As such:

Teacher Leaders must possess the knowledge and skills to lead. Consequently, to be seen as a leader, they must also have a set of positive dispositions and attitudes. Finally, there must be a variety of opportunities for leadership in the school, the district, or larger context. (p. 1)

Within their discussion of skills, they specifically address "knowledge of content and pedagogy" (p. 9). Embedded in this area are many of the skills discussed by the teachers who participated in this study: subject matter knowledge, content and strategies, and mentorship and collaboration. Teacher leadership is best nurtured and sustained when the importance of teacher expertise is recognized and shared at all levels. Embedded within the larger public narrative regarding teacher expertise, there are multiple examples of teachers being treated as one homogenous group with few individual distinctions. In most states, increments in teacher salary are generally dictated by a few variables: experience, advanced degrees, and in a few instances, national board certification. Consequently, within schools, few attempts are made to highlight teacher expertise or the unique talents and training of a few. In fact, in some situations, teachers who possess special areas of expertise and experience are shunned by others who view this recognition and "singling out" as a threat to the larger group of teachers or even an attempt to gain power that is not available to others. Teacher expertise is important to the status of teacher leaders specifically, but more important, to the larger professional status of teachers. The teachers in this study understand the importance of sharing and collaboration within this realm, and yet, there was neither discussion among the participants about how teacher expertise has increased as teachers become better educated nor any references to the relationship between increased expertise (and efficacy) and the professional status of teachers.

4. The Complexities of Power and Decision-Making: Teacher Leadership as an Island

The teachers in this study had many different visions of teacher leadership, but most attempted to reconcile relationships with administrators. At times, they were given an opportunity to "sit at the table" and be involved in decision-making, but other times, expressions of frustration emerged regarding the contradictions in the allocation of power and resources. Feelings of isolation and separation are contrasted with moments of collaboration and communication. The outcomes are emotional, and at times, almost physical in the reactions that are evoked.

> Most of us function as islands. I can ask others for specific help and they will, but their overall attitude is very negative and they spend most group time complaining about the time and resources they

don't have rather than trying to be creative with what is available to us. (#SS)

The P.E. teacher reported to me that our principal once said, "I don't care about specials classes. You're just babysitting until other teachers are back from planning." It was very discouraging to hear about this because it proved to me that the administration did not see me as a professional and rather, I was a "babysitter." (#KR)

I work closely with district leaders. Sometimes, this gives me a big role to play in decision-making for the district and school. Other times, I feel my voice is lost in the sea of mandates and state requirements. Many teachers feel as if they have little say in systemic change. (#OH)

Many of our teachers simply gave up. I had no real say in decision-making at the school. . . . We did nothing for the end of the year incentive and I felt like an idiot in even trying to reach out to the community. Teachers do a lot behind the scenes for their school and for their students. Unfortunately, this goes unseen and unpraised too often. (#KR)

I feel that there is a power struggle between half of the administration team and teachers within the school. Our principal does not seem to get a lot of respect from many teachers who have been with the school since it opened in 2009. (#NB)

Perhaps, there is no other subject that causes more concern and heated discussion of teacher leadership than the issue of power. Simply put, it is all about power, and rather than seeing a sharing of power, the teachers in this study frequently referred to the isolation and distance that seemed to accompany their work as leaders. I return to the quote from Lao Tzu that I previously used, "When the best leaders work is done the people say 'we did it ourselves.'" I often share that quote, people nod their heads in affirmation, and I know in my heart that it means nothing. We are saying the same words, but we are not talking about the collegial and collaborative roles that are behind this quote. The "we" requires collective action, not individual approaches to problem solving. Frequently, I also tell my emerging teacher leaders that you cannot define the problems for a group of people and then tell them the answer. Approaches of this ilk place all of the power in the hands of a few and alienate the perspectives and efforts of the larger group. As such, efforts that require us to build the capacity of an organization for leadership and/or include sustainability in our plans for change are ultimately destined for failure.

Collectively, teachers possess great power; Katzenmeyer and Moller (2001) discuss the "sleeping giant" that is reflected in the power that exists in the expertise and numbers of individuals in the teaching profession. And yet, I believe that there is a pervasive sense of fear and distrust regarding the outcome of awakening that sleeping giant. Again, until there is change within the school culture as a whole, there will only be random and isolated examples of change in the power relationships with educational settings. Democratic and inclusive school settings require a new generation of both teachers and administrators who understand the power of "awakening the sleeping giant" and using that power in the creation of healthier school cultures where collaboration, communication, and higher levels of school achievement become the norm.

"What happens in schools is more complex than ever and cannot be accomplished with strict division between administrators and teachers. The leadership and responsibility for student learning must be a collaborative effort. If teacher leaders can help change school cultures so that teachers and principals collaborate to build a culture of learning, everyone benefits" (Association for Supervision and Curriculum Development, 2014, p. 5). Acker-Hocevar and Touchton (1999) found that "despite expressed frustration with the dynamics of complicated relationships between teachers and administrators, the principal in a school still retains tremendous power to determine both the roles and responsibilities of teachers" (p. 11). The teacher leaders in this study had a lot to say about the management styles of principals and the impact of these styles on their work.

I believe that administration has a bit of a bent toward micromanaging. Teachers do say that administration seems to "question" them about every little detail, making it appear as though the teacher is not trusted to do his/her job. . . . I also believe administration, at times, displays an attitude that test scores are more important than the individual. (#DK)

Decision-making in our school as a whole is done primarily by administration and at the district level. In the classrooms, teachers have a little more say-so when it comes to classroom rules or policies. (#TM)

Decision-making at my school is mostly done by the administrators. We have to go through them to get things done. The role we as teachers play is one where we voice our opinions about things and they listen to us and give us their input. Most of the time it's the final call, no matter if we as teachers don't agree with it. (#KJ)

The status of teacher leadership is clearly reflected in the decision-making that occurs in school setting. Unfortunately, for most teachers, decision-making is limited; however, there are frequent requests for input on important decisions. I am reminded of a statement by a state official many years ago, who informed me that state mandates for more teacher leadership meant that teachers needed to be leaders when implementing the policies, rules, and regulations that govern the work that they do. Nowhere in that statement was there any discussion of how teachers might be involved in the decision-making associated with those policies, rules, and regulations. Acker-Hocevar and Touchton (1999) also found evidence of the chasm between teacher leadership and power relationships, "Power relationships, critical to the change process, can transform or maintain the culture and structures of schools. . . . Teachers cannot be given power (empowered) without accepting it. This has to occur on the part of teacher. On the other hand, administrators must know how to create conditions that foster empowerment and release their control over teachers, alter their roles, and engender commitment, trust, and respect (p. 25). The juxtaposition of these values and beliefs highlight the need to create a context in educational settings where there is value placed on reflection and a re-consideration of the narratives that guide our thinking about the intersection of teacher leadership and real sustainable transformation of school culture.

5. Personal Power, Advocacy, and Social Justice: What's Love Got to Do With It?

When asked to tell stories about personal power, advocacy, and social justice, the teachers in this study did not hesitate to describe a variety of instances where advocacy for their students was central to the work that they do in schools. It is interesting that in the Center for Strengthening the Teaching Profession (CSTP) 2018 document, *Teacher Leadership Skills Framework*, the "equity lens" is a new skill that was added into this more recent document. They describe the knowledge, skills, and dispositions of the "equity lens" in the following manner:

Self and Identity • Becomes aware of own biases, both explicit and implicit • Recognizes the impact of your intentions and position within the system • Seeks new and current skills (lifelong learner)

Understands Race, Power, and Privilege • Seeks to understand historical context, systems of oppression, and their impact on the educational system • Identifies the role in privilege in systems and relationships • Distinguishes between equity versus equality

Understands Intersectionality • Practices and models culturally responsive teaching • Combats institutional "isms" (racism, sexism, ageism, etc.)

Facilitates • Listens intentionally to hear and understand all voices in order to hear and understand perspectives • Questions to encourage equity of voice and participation • Employs mediation skills to navigate discomfort • Facilitates trusting relationships to allow vulnerability and growth • Finds and uses inclusive content and data that invites and encourages discourse

Applies Culturally Relevant and Responsive Practices • Ensures opportunities for all to voice their perspectives • Advocates for equity in terms of access, opportunity, and outcomes • Builds ongoing cultural competence and awareness

Dispositions: • Has courage and commitment to ask hard questions, challenge assumptions, and advocate • Affirms identities and recognizes the power of differences by systematically seeking, valuing, and working with diverse voices and perspectives • Nurtures own social emotional health • Believes in each person's continual need and capacity to grow and change • Sees self as primarily accountable to the community • Self-reflective, empathetic, and compassionate • Understands the limits of one's own perspective (p. 13).

CSTP added the "equity lens" because they believed that while equity is embedded in all of the work done by teacher leaders, "without an intentional focus on equity, Teacher Leaders may unintentionally silo their efforts and therefore risk allowing inequities inherent in the system to persist" (p. 2). The teachers in this study clearly see the knowledge, skills, and dispositions in the area of equity to be important dimensions of their work. The following examples highlight some of the themes from their stories:

I do believe that advocacy and social justice issues are a part of the work that I do. Since I teach a separate classroom, we are often not included in activities that the regular education students are a part of. I routinely have to send emails to the appropriate staff reminding them that our students have the right to the same opportunities that the regular education students have (i.e., field trips, rewards, etc.) and that we need to be included. (#DK)

I do not think of myself as having personal power, other than being positive and building positive relationships with the students. I do advocate for my students by speaking up to other teachers regarding their best interests, and I also support my students when they are advocating for themselves. Keeping our students' best interests in mind at all times is a critical component to what we do as teachers, and I believe keeps us focused on educating them to the best of our abilities and tailored to how they learn best. (#TM)

The needs of students have become greater than the skills of teachers. Though they all love their students and want to see them succeed, they are struggling to reach students with emotional, behavioral, and academic needs. (#OH)

I would say that a large part of accountability would be integrity. (#VM)

Usually the regular education teachers who work with my students have a heart for them and know ways to help them be successful. Most of the "specials" teachers (i.e., music, PE, etc.) also have an understanding of the students I teach. Students are strategically placed with the teachers who have more experience and/or success with the students in my classroom. (#DK)

I am tired of educators trying to reform students or change them when they do not need changing. Students are not empty vessels to be filled with useless facts and garbage. The reason teachers feel they need to change students like this is because teachers are evaluated based upon how "standardized" they can make their children. Our entire teaching career is defined on how we can make students into what they are not. (#KR)

The Center for Strengthening the Teaching Profession (2018) added the "equity lens" to the Teacher Leadership Skills Framework because of the following concerns:

The Framework operates off the assumption that central to Teacher Leader development is the examination of inclusive systems which result in more equitable access, opportunity, representation, and

meaningful participation for individuals with different characteristics, such as race, language proficiency, special education status,
country of origin, gender, or others for educators and students. (p. 2)

The teachers in this study provided numerous examples of how love, commitment, and concern shaped their use of personal power and their advocacy work on behalf of students. Again, it is interesting that teachers are
clear in the values they espouse: integrity, honor, and a commitment to their
students, and yet, they do not tell stories of advocacy for each other and/or
the relationships they have with leadership within the school or within the
larger community. It is even surprising that while the teachers acknowledge
the daily injustices that they confront within their professional lives, they
are hesitant to see themselves as change agents as it might be manifested
in their pedagogical strategies or their work on behalf of larger issues such
as the curriculum and/or class assignment or behavior policies that impact
certain groups of students in negative ways. Advocacy requires a confidence
and a belief in one's power to make changes in areas that have typically
been cut-off from teacher decision-making. And as such, it is not a part of
the stories that they tell.

Discussion, Implications, and Questions: Where Do We Go From Here?

Teacher leadership is not a new concept; it has been around for a while.
However, teacher leadership is politically situated and has often fallen prey
to the whims of "leaders" who want to believe that while teacher leadership
is a powerful concept, it is often defined by the needs of the larger community of individuals who control what goes on in schools; e.g., curriculum,
pedagogy, decision-making, budgets, etc. Silva, Gimbert, and Nolan (2000)
(cited in York-Barr and Duke, 2004) have described three waves of research
on teacher leadership:

In the first wave, teachers served in formal roles (e.g., department
heads, union representatives), essentially as managers, whose main
purpose was to further the efficiency of school operations. In the
second wave, according to Silva and her colleagues, teacher lead-

ership was intended to capitalize more fully on the instructional expertise of teachers by appointing teachers to roles such as curriculum leaders, staff developers, and mentors of new teachers. The third wave of teacher leadership, viewed as emerging currently, recognizes teachers as central to the process of "reculturing" schools such that the intentions of the second wave (i.e., maximizing teachers' instructional expertise) can be realized. (York-Barr & Duke, 2004, p. 261)

York-Barr and Duke acknowledged research from the 1990s that linked teacher leadership to persistent problems with the professional status of teachers, and suggest that "significant investments have been made in educational initiatives focused on improving the quality of teachers and the conditions of teaching" (p. 256). And yet, they cite Yarger and Lee (1994), "who explain that in the absence of conceptual frameworks for guiding program development and evaluation, teacher leadership programs will continue to be sporadic, idiosyncratic events" (p. 235, cited in York-Barr and Duke, 2004, p. 256). York-Barr and Duke propose a theoretical framework to guide practice and inquiry in the area of teacher leadership. Their proposed theoretical framework supports the findings of this study, but falls short of turning the focus in schools on an expanded professional development of teachers that includes a re-visioning of teacher roles and responsibilities. Ultimately, teacher leadership is both a phenomenon and a mind-set regarding the values, beliefs, and attitudes that guide teachers' work, and thus, it has the potential to radically transform a beleaguered profession while also providing for the creation educational spaces that allow for multiple ideologies to coexist and provide multifaceted definitions of efficacy and advocacy in teaching and learning. This research contributes to our understanding of teacher leadership across cultures, how it functions, and what obstacles are still faced by teachers. Principals are important, but their voices have dominated the narrative for too long. It is now time to highlight teacher voice. As such, the voices of the teachers that emerged in this study demonstrate the power of teacher leadership to transform schools, classrooms, and communities, and yet, teachers simultaneously express frustration with at least three aspects of their roles and responsibilities in schools:

- Top-down management that doesn't recognize the educational expertise and professional knowledge of teachers.

- Limited and unequal communication and collaboration between principals and teachers; teachers are not key players in important decision-making activities.

- School culture that was described by one teacher as "rooted in struggle and defeat." Teachers appreciate those schools where there is a sense of family—a team, but other teachers discuss school cultures defined by adversity and distrust among teachers and between teachers and administrators.

Surprisingly, none of the teachers interviewed for this study discussed the larger community beyond the school building; e.g., parents, politicians, and/or community leaders. Teacher leadership, while contributing mightily to the work done in schools and classrooms, nevertheless, still includes an important dimension that is captured by parent advocacy work and communication and collaboration with individuals not directly involved with the schools but impacted by school outcomes. While most of the teachers in this study described themselves as teacher leaders, it is my belief that the educational bureaucracies where these teachers work still reflect a very traditional orientation towards top-down management strategies. Hopefully, there are changes on the horizon. American teachers are becoming more vocal in their complaints about the lack of respect and status afforded their efforts to teach. Certainly the 21st century has presented new educational challenges in the form of changing demographics and the rise of technological innovations that require teachers to be smarter and more creative in their use of innovative research-based strategies that expand the way we think about pedagogy and school-based teaching and learning. Teachers are brilliant, but like birds, they cannot fly if we keep them in a cage and restrict their teaching to 2 x 4 teaching and learning; e.g. the two covers of the textbook and the four walls of the classroom. The teachers in this study are capable and ready, but the stage is not set for the next wave of teacher leadership; the public as well as the leadership of most schools is crippled by a lack of vision. We have to step away from our excuses about "how it used to be" and begin to critically examine where we have been and where we now want to go.

Changing perceptions of teachers' work are paramount to efforts to move the teaching profession towards higher professional status and autonomy—a position that facilitates the emergence of teacher leadership. However, these changes must come from both within the profession and from shifting perceptions that are reflected in the changing bureaucratic and political hierarchies that govern the organization and authority of teachers' work; e.g., relationships must change, both within and beyond the walls of schools.

- Teachers who demonstrate high levels of agency and power in their work simultaneously articulate clear visions of their roles and responsibilities within the school culture as social justice advocates for students, teachers, and families. However, the degree to which school leaders support these roles and responsibilities vary tremendously across school cultures.

- Teachers working in school cultures that facilitate teacher agency and power are more likely to describe their co-workers as a team and view collaboration as an integral part of their work. This aspect of teacher leadership is important, but often neglected in discussions of the process and product of teacher leadership.

Katzenmeyer and Moller (2001) suggest that the future of teacher leadership will only be sustained if we expand career opportunities, provide adequate compensation, improve working conditions, and develop teachers who are advocates for the profession and for change (pp. 124-128). It is a source of concern that for many of the teachers who participated in this study, there were adequate descriptions of the present situation, but few expressions of hope regarding where they would like to be; e.g., what teacher leadership could be under the right circumstances. Teacher leadership for 21st-century schools is something different from teacher leadership in previous decades. Katzenmeyer and Moller (2001) propose that "The status of teachers will be improved when teacher leadership is the norm and when we never again hear the phrase *just a teacher* uttered by a state commissioner of education, a local school board member, a superintendent, or especially by teachers themselves" (p. 124). Within today's schools, teacher leadership must include all of the earlier ideas, but also take a step beyond those definitions of teachers' work and look to a future where teacher leadership is about teachers actively influencing the recreation of both the process and product of teachers' work and the school culture where teachers, principals, and all major stakeholders come together to solve 21st-century problems in education.

References

Acker-Hocevar, M. and Touchton, D. (1999). A Model of Power as Social Relationships: Teacher Leaders Describe the Phenomena of Effective Agency in Practice. Paper presented at the American Educational Research Association Annual Meeting, Montreal, Quebec, Canada. Retrieved from https://files.eric.ed.gov/fulltext/ED456108.pdf

Association for Supervision and Curriculum Development (2014). The what, why and how of teachers as leaders: A report on the fall 2014 ASCD whole child symposium. Report delivered by ASCD Executive Director, Judy Selz. Alexandria, VA: ASCD.

Center for Strengthening the Teaching Profession (CSTP) (2018). Teacher leadership skills framework. Retrieved from http://www.cstp-wa.org

Colaizzi, P. (1978). Psychological research as the phenomenologist views it. In Ronald S. Valle and Mark King (Eds.), *Existential-phenomenological alternatives for psychology*. New York: Oxford University Press.

Covey, S. (2013). The 7 habits of highly successful people: Powerful lessons in personal change (Anniversary Edition). New York: Simon & Schuster.

Katzenmeyer, M., & Moller, G. (2001). *Awakening the sleeping giant: Helping teachers develop as leaders* (2nd ed.). Thousand Oaks, CA: Corwin Press.

North Carolina Professional Teaching Standards. (2008). North Carolina Department of Public Instruction. Raleigh, N.C. Retrieved from http://www.ncpublicschools.org/docs/profdev/standards/teachingstandards.pdf

North Carolina Professional Teaching Standards. (2013). North Carolina Department of Public Instruction. Raleigh, NC. Retrieved from http://www.ncpublicschools.org/docs/effectiveness-model/ncees/standards/prof-teach-standards.pdf

Schlechty, P. C. (1993, Fall). On the frontier of school reform with trailblazers, pioneers, and settlers. *Journal of Staff Development, 14*(4), pp. 46–51.

Silva, D. Y., Gimbert, B., & Nolan, J. (2000). Sliding the doors: Locking and unlocking possibilities for teacher leadership. *Teachers College Record, 102*(4), 779–804.

Yarger, S. J., & Lee, O. (1994). The development and sustenance of instructional leadership. In D. R. Walling (Ed.), *Teachers as leaders: Perspectives on the professional development of teachers* (pp. 223–237). Bloomington, IN: Phi Delta Kappa Educational Foundation.

York-Barr, J., & Duke, K. (2004). What do we know about teacher leadership? Findings from two decades of scholarship. *Review of Educational Research, 74*(3), pp. 255–316.

CHAPTER NINE

Teacher Leadership for 21st-Century Schools:

An Old Wine in a New Bottle?

Eleanor J. Blair

It's funny to me that when I think about schools, I often muse about my personal history with schools. In 1960, as a first grader, I came home with my report card, my first report card, and on the back the teacher had written, "Eleanor Jane never smiles." My parents, as all good parents would, promptly asked me why I didn't smile at school. My oft-repeated response was, "There's nothing to smile about at school"; everyone who heard that story laughed; it really wasn't a funny story, it was kind of sad, but that wasn't the focus of the adults I came in contact with during those days. Recently, I came across that report card, and yes, I must be a hoarder of sorts, but it set me to thinking about schools. Are schools really such somber places, that there is nothing to smile about in that context? Almost 60 years ago, in my innocence, I believed that to be true. And now, all these years later, I sit and wonder if it is still true. Are schools dreary places of confinement and drudgery for both teachers and students? Is it unreasonable to think that both teachers and students could thrive, find fulfillment, and even laughter within the walls of those schools? I know that I go out to some schools and I am lifted up by the excitement and enthusiasm I encounter, but at other schools, not so much. Some schools are literally defined by the unhappiness that seems to pervade their walls; students and teachers are not happy and it shows in their relationships with each other. So, as I write this book and consider teachers within a larger historical context, I am forced to ask, why? Why are teachers still struggling with the same issues that that were part and parcel of a teaching career 150 years ago? Doctors and lawyers have successfully achieved higher professional status; why not teachers? No clear answers to these questions exist, although teaching has always been unique in the sense that teachers are seen as public servants with little autonomy and few opportunities to control who enters the profession. It can be hoped that with higher educational requirements for entry into the profession, increased levels of accountability, greater opportunities to assume leadership positions within the profession and participate in important decision-making activities, the teaching profession could see a transformation in the breadth, depth, and scope of teachers' work in the 21st century. Yet, still teaching is stymied by multiple influences, both professional and political, that are powerful. Expectations and biases associated with a profession dominated by women have not helped, but teachers are better educated and more important than ever, and yet, each step forward seems to be accompanied by two steps back.

While the North Carolina Professional Teaching Standards provides guidelines for teachers, the North Carolina Standards for School Executives (2006) presents a different side of the same coin. These standards open with the charge that 21st-century schools require a vision of a new kind of school leader, an executive rather than an administrator (p. 1). Principals are provided eight standards of executive leadership that range from instructional to cultural to academic achievement leadership tasks; the standards are comprehensive and include myriad tasks and responsibilities. In addition to the standards, the report delineates the basic competencies that are critical to supporting multiple leadership behaviors. More relevant to teachers' work is the principal's role in creating an environment that supports and facilitates leadership capacity building among stakeholders:

> The successful work of the new executive will only be realized in the creation of a culture in which leadership is distributed and encouraged with teachers, which consists of open, honest communication, which is focused on the use of data, teamwork, research-based best practices, and which uses modern tools to drive ethical and princi-

pled, goal-oriented action. This culture of disciplined thought and action is rooted in the ability of the relationships among all stakeholders to build a trusting, transparent environment that reduces all stakeholders' sense of vulnerability as they address the challenges of transformational change. (p. 1)

If teacher leadership is both a phenomenon and a mind-set regarding the values, beliefs, and attitudes that guide teachers' work then principal leadership is an equally, if not more, important mind-set regarding the values, beliefs, and attitudes that guide principals' work. Within this context, the report clearly stipulates the beliefs and values that are important dimensions of the standards presented. Of the eleven stated values and beliefs, several intersect with the work to teacher leaders. For example,

- Leadership is not a position or a person. It is a practice that must be embedded in all job roles at all levels of the school district.

- The work of leadership is about working with, for, and through people. It is a social act. Whether we are discussing instructional leadership, change leadership, or leadership as learning, people are always the medium for the leader.

- Leadership is not about doing everything oneself but it is always about creating processes and systems that will cause everything to happen.

- Leadership is about setting direction, and aligning and motivating people to implement positive sustained improvement. (pp. 1-2)

Inherent to this philosophy are notions about distributed leadership and creating a more democratic and inclusive environment for the tasks associated with teaching and learning. However, despite a supportive philosophical orientation and both teacher and school standards that seem to support teacher leadership, there is no clear delineation of how the emergence of a culture that supports teacher leadership will differ from the status quo. More importantly, there is little acknowledgement of required resources and/or barriers to teacher leadership. Clearly there is a vision in place with few structures for facilitating, nurturing, or sustaining teacher leadership. Those who seem to have the most power over teachers, politicians, educational leaders, and the general public seem unwilling to recognize the strides that have been made within the profession. Teachers are on the cusp of what could be a major transformation of the profession, and yet, the progress is slow and uneven.

It is interesting to consider that if principals are moving into new roles as school executives, perhaps, it would be equally appropriate to conceptualize 21st-century teacher leaders as pedagogical executives. A Google search of the term *executive* provides the following definition, "having the power to put plans, actions, or laws into effect." Whereas, Dictionary.com (n.d.) defines executives as "persons or a group of persons having administrative of supervisory authority in an organization" (n.p.). It seems inconceivable to *not* consider that teachers, as experts in pedagogy; i.e., the art, science, and profession of teaching, should have the power and authority to lead and supervise the work of teaching and learning in most educational contexts. Using the same language that appeared in the North Carolina Standards for School Executives (2006) to describe the work of school executives, it is relatively easy to view pedagogical executives as individuals participating in:

> The creation of a culture in which leadership is distributed and encouraged with teachers, which consists of open, honest communication, which is focused on the use of data, teamwork, research-based best practices, and which uses modern tools to drive ethical and principled, goal-oriented action. This culture of disciplined thought and action is rooted in the ability of the relationships among all stakeholders to build a trusting, transparent environment that reduces all stakeholders' sense of vulnerability as they address the challenges of transformational change. (p. 1)

Of far more concern is the fact that it seems easy to think of school executives in these kinds of roles, but for teachers, there was only one standard related to teacher leadership. Thinking of teachers as pedagogical executives refocuses the discussion on teachers as professionals possessing special expertise in pedagogical knowledge, skills, and reflection. The term *peda-*

gogical executive connotes a different kind of role for teachers within the bureaucracy. As such, I challenge teachers to begin thinking of themselves in the same ways that principals or school executives have begun thinking of themselves. Perhaps, 21st-century schools require a vision of a new kind of teacher leader, an executive rather than simply a teacher. Regardless of whether teachers are viewed as pedagogical executives or not, Acker-Hocevar and Touchton (1999) concluded that:

> "principals must find authentic ways to support teachers, not to increase their stress through surveillance and micro-management techniques. These administrative actions neither build professional teacher cultures, nor improve practice. Rather, principals should err on the side of promoting risk-taking, seeking to address teacher and student needs that focus on teaching and learning. Principals might play a buffering role in protecting teachers from unnecessary pressures from their districts and the state. They could seek to build collective agency, reflective practice, and common planning times for teacher dialogue. Principals can foster development by focusing on the internal strengths of their staffs, negotiate external demands that are stressful, and provide opportunities for growth. By providing an open-minded stance that enables teachers and administrators to listen to each other, educators can learn together" (p. 25).

And at the end of the day, collaborative relationships and open communication is the bedrock of school improvement through a re-alignment of both teacher and administrative roles and responsibilities.

Teacher leadership is important because there is no other job in society that is more important than teaching and guiding the children who enter our schools each year full of hope and optimism. Teachers are the key to making schools work, and yet, that message falls on "deaf ears" among those charged with making the most important decisions about schools. Teachers acting as leaders is important. Questions about teachers' work and teacher leadership are related to teaching and learning and school reform in profound ways. The findings from research by York-Barr and Duke (2004) support the findings of this study in profound ways. Listed below are a few of the most relevant examples:

- Teacher leadership is an umbrella term that includes a wide variety of work at multiple levels in educational systems, including work with students, colleagues, and administrators and work that is focused on instructional, professional, and organizational development.

- Teacher leaders have backgrounds as accomplished teachers, and they are respected by their colleagues. From this background, they extend their knowledge, skills, and influence to others in their school communities.

- Teacher leadership roles are often ambiguous. The likelihood of being successful as a teacher leader is increased if roles and expectations are mutually shaped and negotiated by teacher leaders, their colleagues, and principals on the basis of context-specific (and changing) instructional and improvement needs.

- Professional norms of isolation, individualism, and egalitarianism challenge the emergence of teacher leadership. Teachers who lead tend to feel conflict and isolation as the nature of their collegial relationships shifts from primarily horizontal to somewhat hierarchical.

- Developing trusting and collaborative relationships is the primary means by which teacher leaders influence their colleagues.

- Principals play a pivotal role in the success of teacher leadership by actively supporting the development of teachers, by maintaining open channels of communication, and by aligning structures and resources to support the leadership work of teachers.

- The most consistently documented positive effects of teacher leadership are on the teacher leaders themselves, supporting the belief that leading and learning are interrelated. Teacher leaders grow in their understanding of instructional, professional, and organizational practice as they lead. Less empirical evidence supports student, collegial, and school-level effects. (p. 288)

The aforementioned themes intersected and supported the findings from the current research project and provided a larger context for viewing the narratives that emerged from this study. While York-Barr and Duke (2004) succinctly summarized previous quantitative work on this topic, the teachers who were interviewed in this study lend a "voice" to the ideas captured in earlier work. It is my fervent belief that each of the 12 people who participated in this study have the skill and talent to take key leadership roles in 21st-century schools, and yet, the journey will require a clear vision—a sense of what the "end" looks like for teachers. What do we want the teaching profession to look like in the 21st century? And more importantly, how do we close the gap between where teachers are today and where they need to be in the future? What work needs to be done? What concessions have to be negotiated? I believe that a new generation of principals and educational leaders have the power to create new spaces for teacher leaders to thrive, but will this happen without a push from below by teachers? I believe that it is inevitable that 21st-century schools and the teaching profession will change, but change without a map or clearly defined destination may not be the type of positive change that teachers and schools deserve in a world where education and schooling is more important than ever before.

As I consider the current status of teacher leadership, I am forced to consider that the work of teacher leaders is stymied by issues of power and invisibility. There seems to be an implicit desire for teachers to be overwhelmingly compliant and more often seen, but not heard. And yet, how do we begin to address issues of powerlessness and invisibility? Teachers, as a group, in the fall, 2018, represented 3.2 million individuals who work in K-12 public institutions (National Center for Education Statistics, n.d., n.p.). Teachers working together through unions and other professional affiliations must seek ways to assert their power and take steps to guide the profession in new and empowering ways. It is unfortunate that public visibility of teachers' work is often presented in negative ways; teachers appear on covers of magazines and in newspaper articles when they are being highlighted for behavior that evokes public scrutiny of teachers in ways that do not always move the conversation forward regarding raising the professional status of teachers; e.g., teacher moonlighting, public school crises, low test scores, etc. Efforts to establish national governing boards and higher standards for teacher preparation and even mediated entry into the profession are all tools that have been discussed without significantly changing the nature of teachers' work. It was interesting that among the teachers interviewed for this study, teachers have many concerns and complaints about entry into the profession, mentorship and leadership, but yet, they don't have the language and/or the tools to begin talking about solutions. For example, without adequate preparation and training, teachers do not have a context for talking about the professional status of teaching and changing roles and responsibilities entailed by various forms of leadership. Teacher preparation has most often been for the purpose of entering a semi-profession where voice, activism, and resistance were seldom encouraged. The tools for making demands for greater professional status and mediating disputes were not provided. As such, teachers may have a vision for teacher leadership, but lack the skills to make it happen.

I am certain that I do not have the answers to the dilemmas faced by teachers attempting to find acceptance and support for their leadership efforts, but I know that a consideration of the concerns and issues that emerge are important to this discussion. I don't want to believe that teacher leadership is simply an "old wine in a new bottle," but perhaps, it would be acceptable to consider teacher leadership as an old wine that has aged and developed a richness and complexity that requires a new marketing strategy. I say this "tongue in cheek," but behind my humor is some degree of truth. Teachers' work and the teaching profession suffer from being perceived as a place where powerlessness and invisibility are a part of the job. Teachers are celebrated as powerful, influencing agencies in the lives of children, and yet, teacher demands for higher professional status are dismissed as irrelevant to the progress and status of American education. Teacher leadership is not simply a personal issue; it is about making schools and education inclusive environments for all people; it is about supporting democratic values of equity, freedom, and justice for all. Recent teacher strikes have been met with commentary that reflects a "you knew what you were getting when you became a teacher, why expect more" mentality. And as I frequently tell my students, if you have ever played "King of the Mountain" as a child, you should not forget the lesson; people will fight to retain power. So, where does this leave teachers? How do you fight if you are invisible and lacking power? In my mind, a quote from Frederick Douglass (1857) has relevance to this discussion:

> If there is no struggle there is no progress. Those who profess to favor freedom and yet deprecate agitation, are men who want crops without plowing up the ground, they want rain without thunder

and lightning. They want the ocean without the awful roar of its many waters. This struggle may be a moral one, or it may be a physical one, and it may be both moral and physical, but it must be a struggle. Power concedes nothing without a demand. It never did and it never will. (p. 437)

The progress of teacher leaders working on behalf of the profession as a whole and not just school improvement is a personal struggle that requires that teachers be "seen" and that their struggles for power and autonomy be acknowledged and legitimized by those with power and authority over the work of teachers. And yet, simultaneously, this is a struggle that requires a re-negotiation of power relationships within the educational bureaucracy. As Douglass laments, "Power concedes nothing without a demand," and as such, teachers will not be simply given a "place at the table" where powerful decisions are made regarding the roles and responsibilities of teachers. Simultaneously, demands will be made of teachers' time and teachers' work, and demands for visibility must come from all teachers, not just a few. Wide-scale participation in the struggle to make the profession what it can be, what it should be and what it must be if 21st-century schools are going to make meaningful changes in the process and product of education must occur. Thus, those who advocate for teacher leadership, but view with disdain the additional work and time required to move the profession forward, are people who want the benefits of higher professional status, but not the discomfort that is prerequisite to progress. Progress is seldom silent and steady, but more often loud and chaotic.

Emergent teacher leadership has the power to transform the work of teachers both in and out of the classroom; it has the power to transform schools into public spaces where egalitarian values of inclusiveness and advocacy are the norm. However, the relinquishment (or sharing) of power from the status quo will not occur without a struggle. York-Barr and Duke (2004) emphasized that principals do play a pivotal role in supporting the work of teacher leaders, but the time has come for teachers to play an equally important role in pushing for greater participation in major decision-making that impacts the profession; e.g., teacher training, licensure, entry into the profession, allocation of resources, curriculum, and pedagogy. In an ideal world, teachers would be represented on boards and policy commissions, ad hoc groups, etc. Teachers in 21st-century schools must actively lobby on behalf of their own self-interests as well as those of the families and students they represent. Barth (2001) asserted that just as all students can learn, "All teachers can lead. Indeed, if schools are going to become places in which all students are learning, all teachers must lead" (p. 444). Obviously, this kind of action requires that teachers, as a group, be willing to become activists that refuse to look away from the precarious position of the profession today. The circumstances today are unique in that schools (and teachers) are regularly failing to meet the demands of an increasingly diverse, technological society where K-12 education is being closely scrutinized. Teachers' work is at a crossroads; the profession has the opportunity to move forward or backwards, but who will direct that progress and what will that struggle look like for those in positions of power? Historically, it was accepted that teachers operated behind the scenes with minimal power; and as such, they were occasionally portrayed as self-sacrificing martyrs who tirelessly worked on behalf of their students. The expectations for teachers' work were high with few inducements to work towards higher professional status and the rewards that typically accompany the work of doctors or lawyers.

In closing, I want to return to the idea that schools have the potential to be joyous places characterized by educational critique and argument, and opportunities for success and self-determination by teachers acting as leaders. And yes, I have visited schools that represent that kind of environment; however, I have also recently visited schools where the lines between teachers and administrators are sharply drawn with distrust and cynicism guiding the actions on both sides. Even in the best schools, I am often dismayed by the lack of communication and collaboration among teachers and administrators; teachers are "allowed" to participate in discussions about important decisions, but ultimately, they are reminded that teachers don't make the final decisions; people with power make the decisions and teachers don't have much power beyond individual classrooms. The "voices" from the teachers who participated in this study confirmed this perspective repeatedly, and yet, for most, there was an acceptance that complicity and conformity was not only expected, but rewarded. If this book does nothing else, it is hoped that it will remind teachers that while teachers' work is always challenging, they must seek opportunities to demonstrate what teachers' work should look like in the 21st century. Teachers' work, by necessity, should provide a space for for collaboration and communication of a vision that contributes to the creation of school cultures that nurture the collegiality necessary to encourage and support teacher leadership while building the sustainability of high performing schools. Again, a vision is needed, and hopefully, the teachers who participated in this study have "opened the doors" to in-depth discussions about teachers' work. In the end, the struggle must be real and an acknowledgement of the many dimensions of that struggle must be a daily part of the process and product of teacher leadership if progress is going to be made.

References

Acker-Hocevar, M. and Touchton, D. (1999). A Model of Power as Social Relationships: Teacher Leaders Describe the Phenomena of Effective Agency in Practice. Paper presented at the American Educational Research Association Annual Meeting, Montreal, Quebec, Canada. Retrieved from https://files.eric.ed.gov/fulltext/ED456108.pdf

Barth, R. (2001). Teacher leader. *Phi Delta Kappan, 82*(6), 443–449.

Dictionary.com (n.d.). Retrieved from https://www.dictionary.com/browse/executive

Douglass, F. (1857). West India Emancipation. Speech delivered at Canandaigua, New York, August 4, 1857. Cited in Douglass, F. (Author) and Foner, E. (Ed.) (1950). *The life and writings of Frederick Douglass* (Volume 2): Pre-Civil War Decade, 1850-1860. p. 437.

National Center for Education Statistics (n.d.). Retrieved from https://nces.ed.gov/fastfacts/display.asp?id=372

North Carolina Professional Teaching Standards. (2008). North Carolina Department of Public Instruction. Raleigh, N.C. Retrieved from http://www.ncpublicschools.org/docs/profdev/standards/teachingstandards.pdf

North Carolina Standards for School Executives. (2006). North Carolina Department of Public Instruction. Raleigh, N.C. Retrieved from http://www.ncpublic schools.org/docs/profdev/training/standards/executivestandards/principals.pdf

York-Barr, J., & Duke, K. (2004). What do we know about teacher leadership? Findings from two decades of scholarship. *Review of Educational Research, 74*(3), 255–316.

Cross-Cultural Considerations of Teacher Leaders' Work

CHAPTER TEN

Cross-Cultural Conversations About Teacher Leadership:

Reflections on Trends That Transcend Culture

CARMEL ROOFE, ELEANOR J. BLAIR, AND SUSAN TIMMINS

UNDOUBTEDLY TEACHER LEADERSHIP IS a necessity for 21st-century school improvement and a redefinition of teachers' roles and responsibilities across borders and cultures as members of the teaching profession. However, for all countries to benefit from teacher leadership, there is need for increased awareness of its benefits in shaping school cultures and impacting not only the teaching profession, but overall school improvement. The three countries examined in this project all seem to be at a critical point where more work needs to be done to develop the relationships needed to transform school cultures and create contexts where teacher leadership can "awaken the sleeping giant" of power and resources in the domain of teachers' work. For Jamaica, this is a critical and urgent undertaking given the wave of ongoing school, and, curriculum reform being undertaken to support VISION 2030, which aims to make Jamaica the place of choice, to live, work, raise families, and do business. Achieving this vision requires collaborative leadership that holds each group of stakeholders accountable for their individual and collective roles. In the United States and England, attention needs to be given to mitigating challenges posed by political structures that seek to erode the strides made in creating awareness of the benefits of teacher leadership.

Recent trends and critiques of education and schooling in each of the three countries examined, indicate a growing need for schools to be a tool for addressing changes in demographics as well as the challenges of a global, technologically advanced society requiring workers with new and very different cognitive and technical skills. Since teachers' roles are linked to the transformation of society, their work as leaders within the teaching profession remains a starting point for shifting mindsets (Eteläpelto, Vähäsantanen, Hökkä, & Paloniemi, 2013; Miller, 1999).

This research looked at teacher leadership in three very different countries. A standard interview protocol was used by each of the principal investigators to probe the thinking about teacher leadership by each of the participants interviewed. Interviews from 36 teachers—12 in each country—were conducted and subjected to a phenomenological analysis that produced categories of themes to extract the most salient ideas from the interviews. A summary of the themes used to discuss the findings in each country is presented in Table 10.1.

Table 10.1: Themes used to discuss findings in England, Jamaica, United States

England (Timmins)	Jamaica (Roofe)	United States (Blair)
• Caring beyond the classroom • Agency and power • The ceiling effect • Steering through the politics • Relationships: In with the in crowd • Culture: You get out what you put in • Value teacher expertise	• Characteristics of teacher leaders in Jamaica and what they value • The nexus between principal leadership, school ethos, and teacher leadership • Nature of teacher leaders' work • Context matters in teacher leaders' work • Challenges to teacher leaders' work • Agency amidst difficulties	• Career dilemmas: Becoming a teacher • School culture: We are family • Flavors of teacher leadership • The complexities of power and decision-making: Teacher leadership as an island • Personal power, advocacy, and social justice: What's love got to do with it?

The themes provide a mechanism for comparing and contrasting the findings that emerged from the research, and while language varies, it reveals some of the similarities among the three countries. Some of these commonalities were the following: caring and concern about relationships between teachers, families, and students; issues related to school culture; concerns about hierarchical power structures, politics, and decision-making; and finally, a consideration of the intersection of teacher expertise and the kinds of roles "played" by teacher leaders. From this project, it was evident that there are elements of teacher leadership that transcend specific school and country contexts despite the fact that the enactment in each of these countries varied based on differences in school structure and organization as well as historical precedents. The studies conducted in England, Jamaica, and the United States highlighted that teachers' work is highly political and that the political structures within the educational bureaucracy often create the differences in how teacher leadership is enacted. In this section of the book, we will highlight some of the issues and concerns that emerged as well as provide a platform for the authors to share their personal reflections on the future of teacher leadership.

One of the challenges for teacher leadership across the three countries is the power struggle or tensions between school administrators/leaders and teachers that often cripple school improvement and professional development efforts. Attention must be given to deconstructing and designing strategies to solve this issue as it was prevalent in each of the three countries. The power struggle/tensions led to unhealthy alliances in schools and impeded collaboration and communication across all major stakeholders. Linked to this challenge was the division amongst staff based on decision-making protocols and suspicions about how power and agency manifested itself throughout the school context; concerns were regularly expressed about favoritism and nepotism. Though teacher leaders in all three countries found ways to maneuver these alliances, their existence led to a lack of objectivity when a decision needed to be made and teachers took sides to support a person rather than an initiative. Challenges to school improvement such as these align with Bacharach's (1983) view that schools are political systems and members are political players with their own needs, objectives, and approaches to achieve those objectives (p. 10). Notwithstanding these views, the needs of students should be the center of all decision-making in schools. Personal subjectivities must give way to a focus on what will best support students' needs given a particular context. Given what is required of 21st-century school leaders to improve schools, effective leadership cannot be bound in a person or be singular, but must be distributed amongst other stakeholders within the school community (Harris, 2002). Birthing new teacher leaders in contexts such as these requires influencing mindsets so that teachers and administrators learn to put differences aside for the greater good of improved student outcomes.

Another important observation from the studies that is worthy of mention in this cross-cultural conversation is the role that monetary compensation plays in defining leadership in schools. In trying to retain good staff, teachers in England receive monetary rewards for additional duties and teachers in the United States regularly seek out additional compensation for any additional duties; however, this is not the case in Jamaica. And yet, research on teacher moonlighting (Blair, 2018) has shown that while additional compensation is helpful, it is usually minimal and does not address teacher concerns about working conditions that stifle attempts by teachers to demonstrate autonomy and participate in decision-making. Monetary compensation therefore if not managed appropriately could serve as an obstacle to teacher leadership emerging as an inherent component of the roles and responsibilities of all teachers. While we all know that monetary rewards are important, the teacher leaders across the three countries highlighted that they placed more significance on feelings of being valued and appreciated for their work. This suggests that monetary rewards alone won't solve the problem of the need for increased teacher leadership, and under more favorable circumstances, monetary rewards must be coupled with other tangible ways of recognizing and valuing teacher leaders' work.

In particular, the research in England documented that the practice of giving teachers autonomy coupled with monetary compensation led to better relations and improved school outcomes. The practice shared by one of the teacher leaders was the approach administrators took to making decisions about ongoing professional development for staff. For staff at this school, they were asked to indicate their professional development needs. Having done so, a list of professional sessions was generated from which staff could select the preferred session to be undertaken based on their needs, at a given time. As such, teachers were motivated to attend sessions based on their needs, rather than being told what sessions to attend. This method gives teachers a much needed "voice" in assessing their strengths and weaknesses and making autonomous decisions about the skills they want to develop. Such a practice, we believe, places the professional responsibility on the teacher and sends the message to the teacher that "you know best what you need to empower you." This shows a valuing of the teacher as a professional and disrupts a narrative where teachers are told their problems and then given a solution by someone who has the power and authority to dominate those conversations. Such a practice also showcases an example of a shared leadership approach to decision-making—one of the approaches teacher leaders in the study felt was missing from how many of the schools in which they worked were led. Utilizing this shared approach and involving teachers in leading some of these sessions at the school level is also a mechanism whereby principals can empower their staff at the whole school level. Across the three countries, teachers felt empowered to initiate change or to utilize their expertise at departmental, grade, or class levels, but seldom at a whole school level. Principals of schools therefore need to develop a strategy for ascertaining the skills of those whom they lead and how to utilize those skills to help lead school improvement.

Beyond the Voices of the 36 Teacher Leaders

Beyond the voices of the 36 teacher leaders in this project, we now turn to a more informal conversation to share our perspectives about teacher leadership in the 21st century and to demonstrate that the conversation needs to continue. We use the following three questions to guide our informal conversation.

1. Is it possible to equalize power relationships in a school culture so that teachers and principals have equal professional status and their relationships are defined by respect, collaboration, and mutual decision-making?

2. How do we "disrupt" the status quo and use the information from this study as a foundation for the transformation of school cultures?

3. Is there an intersection between agency and power and the experience, education, and personal attributes of individual teachers? If so, how do

we facilitate and nurture the professional development of all teachers so that teacher leadership is the norm, not the exception?

Eleanor notes, sometimes I worry that despite the personal and professional advantages of the emergence of teacher leadership as the status quo in teachers' work, I am not sure that teachers are ready to be leaders. There will always be teachers who are ready to do something new, take the helm, lead others in achieving a new initiative, but for many, change is challenging, and at times, threatening. Some teachers love teaching not because they wanted to change the world, but rather, because they want that part of the world to stay the same; they don't want change. They want to teach, and they want students to learn. Showing up and doing the work each day is fine, but don't ask everyone to do more, be more in their role as a teacher. In contemporary schools, I do believe that we have principals and teachers who are ready to embrace changes in the school culture and the leadership of the school. However, the biggest obstacles come in the form of other teachers and parents.

As Philip Schlechty (1993) has observed, there will be within any school environment, individuals who are ready to take the risks and lead the "charge," but there will also be the saboteurs who are waiting to "shame and blame" those who tried to make changes to the status quo. I often tell emerging teacher leaders, "Keep your friends close, but your enemies closer"; those who are waiting to applaud your failures cannot be allowed to stop the work of innovators, but they must also be watched carefully to avert efforts to stop change by nurturing dissent and dissatisfaction among other staff and the community. Teacher leadership requires skillful preparation and it takes an insightful, and perhaps brilliant, administrator to recognize how to prepare, nurture, and sustain the fledgling efforts of novice teacher leaders. In the end, when teacher leaders flourish, everyone wins; school improvement and the development of teachers as both learners and leaders transform schools in ways that create an inviting school culture for all stakeholders.

Finally, my frustration with progress is that it is so slow and often feels as if each step forward is accompanied by two backwards. I don't see teacher leadership being "part and parcel" of principal AND teacher preparation, and as such, principals who try to empower teachers are often seen as weak by other teachers and administrators. A lack of understanding of how collaboration works within schools operating as professional learning communities (PLCs) is evident in many of my discussions with teachers. For many individuals, PLCs are seen as an extra layer of work in institutions that are dominated by historical precedents that guide relationships and the work required to "grow" schools that are responsive to rapidly changing demands from students, families, and communities. Schools should be dynamic institutions capable of expanding and contracting to meet the needs of society, but the opposite is often the reality. Rather than reflecting the latest research on best practices, educators seem to be constantly looking over their shoulders at the "way it has always been done." Too often in education, innovation and change is viewed with suspicion. I cannot imagine doctors viewing new medicine and innovative treatments with the same level of skepticism, and yet, in education we celebrate tradition and view with disdain the kinds of changes that could radically transform practice and create schools where high achievement AND teacher leadership is the norm.

Carmel posits that it is possible to equalize power relationships defined by respect, collaboration, and culture, but much work needs to be done for this to be sustained. Based on my 24 years of being in the teaching profession and interacting with school personnel, I believe one of the challenges facing schools is the act of making such power relations sustainable. I believe that for teachers and principals to have equal professional status in schools in Jamaica, both principals and teachers must first interrogate their individual past history of how teaching and principalship started in Jamaica, and how their roles are situated in this history as members of a profession. From my experience with interacting with those who work in schools, the issue that seems to prevent a sustained sense of equal power relations is that of mistrust. Teachers do not seem to trust the principals, principals do not trust teachers, and both do not trust the system of governance of which they are a part.

There is also something that I have been reflecting on that I find paradoxical about my colleagues in the teaching profession. I find we often cast blame on the politicians for "mashing up" the system of which we are a part, yet we still look to them and not ourselves to "fix" the system. In other words, we are always looking to others rather than ourselves as teachers to agitate for us and implement the solutions we desire. I believe that within this era of the teaching profession, a new wave of consciousness needs to spread amongst teachers so that we begin to utilize a bottom up advocacy approach to influence the change we desire in the profession. For example, how about teachers agitating for change in how unions, such as the Jamaica Teachers Association, advocates for them? What if the unions, in addition to wage negotiations, which are critical to teachers' realities, advocate for better working conditions for teachers, increased timely access to resources to support students, appropriately planned professional development sessions, etc. with the same vigor and exuberance they use for increased salaries? What if the central ministry in Jamaica utilized more opportunities in the media to thank and praise teachers and talk more about teachers who have been doing well? Or what if news reporters investigated and reported more of the positive happenings in teachers' work in schools? As one of my graduate students noted in one of our recent class discussions, "Teaching is the most ungrateful profession in Jamaica," to which almost all of her 27 classmates applauded. At the heart of such comment is the undervaluing and lack of appreciation of their work. As teachers, we can begin to disrupt the status quo owning our professional responsibilities. There are teachers who are friends with colleagues who are leaders in schools, but as leaders, they do not act in professional ways and we fail to hold them accountable as friends. Let's turn the search light on ourselves and see where we fall short and take actions that take away from our value.

As I bring my comments to a close, I note though that there is no one-size-fits-all approach to disrupting the status quo. Each school with each principal with each teacher must interrogate the context for him/herself and then be willing to share the findings from this interrogation with each other. There must also be a willingness to listen to each other as we think through the solutions and the actions needed to derive the solutions. Each must hold each other accountable for arriving at the solutions. In other words, embedded in this is a school-based bottom up approach to disrupting the status quo. Teachers need to see themselves first as persons who can be the change as opposed to looking for someone else to be the change.

Though the Jamaican study was not designed to ascertain how teacher leaders derived the traits they possessed, from their narratives it seems that for some their actions of agency emanated from negative educational and personal experiences, while for others it was their personal/innate trait being brought out by the context in which they found themselves working. Considering this, nurturing the professional development of all teachers so that teacher leadership becomes the norm and not the exception is a complex undertaking but not an impossible one. Such undertaking requires a paradigm shift in how schools and those who work in them are thought about by parents, students, and the average citizen. It also requires a paradigm shift in how teachers and principals think and feel about themselves and their work. Teachers in Jamaica have been cultured to be docile and helpless as professionals waiting and ready to implement the next policy directive. Even where teachers do not act docile there are leaders and policymakers who perpetuate this perception. Additionally, in some schools where teachers do not subscribe to that mold, they face a myriad of challenges and are sometimes demonized by their colleagues. I believe this speaks to the elitist structure of our education system in Jamaica where a subtle system of othering is perpetuated. As noted by Marcus Garvey, "it is by education that we become prepared for our duties and responsibilities in life. If one is badly educated, he must naturally fail in the proper assumption and practice of his duties and responsibilities" (Garvey, M., 1986, p. 98). As a teacher educator preparing in-service teachers at the graduate level, too often teachers are willing to articulate and expound on the many problems in schools, but oftentimes not willing to spend time co-constructing possible solutions. This may be part of our culture as a people or a natural tendency of humanity—I am not sure. It therefore means that professional development for teachers must include strategies for shifting mental conceptualizations and their premises. Professional development must challenge the assumptions teachers hold and help them, where necessary, to form new assumptions, those needed to see themselves as leaders. Hence to make teacher leadership the norm, we have to embrace a new wave of how schooling and the curriculum in schools is structured and how teachers are trained for the profession. Furthermore, to make teacher leadership the norm and not the exception, teachers need to heed these two lines from Bob Marley's redemption song, *emancipate yourselves from mental slavery, none but ourselves can free our minds*. In other words, teachers need to begin to disrupt the narrative that they are "just" implementers of policy ideals and that they do not possess solutions to fix the circumstances in their schools. Disrupting the status quo begins with each teacher, as teachers are the ones who ultimately become principals in schools in Jamaica. While teachers do not exercise all the control over the education system, I believe that if more teachers begin to change their thinking, the other support subsystems for their work will begin to change for the better. However, teachers need to understand as well that this is not an easy fix or an overnight fix, and so they must demonstrate the spirit of perseverance as shared by the teachers in the Jamaican study. It starts with a willingness from each teacher to do more and for teachers collectively to demonstrate through their actions a long-term commitment to transforming school cultures into professional learning communities where collaborative relationships regularly nurture, support, and sustain teacher leadership.

In adding to the conversation, Susan states, I dream that it is possible to equalise the power relationships in our school cultures, to have places where teachers and head teachers share a mutual respect and share responsibilities and decision-making for the good of the school community. It is evident that slow progress has been made over the last decade in the realm of teacher leadership; however, it is heartening to see glimmers of hope and transformations taking place in some schools and academies in England. Where this transformational shift has occurred, it has been driven by the senior management within these organisations, and they have been successful in establishing a culture of professional enquiry, developed structures which enable teacher leaders to lead, and have provided opportunities for collaboration within the school and beyond. The senior management in these cases recognize the value of teacher leadership within their organisations and they are beginning to share leadership responsibilities and decision-making with others. Some head teachers and senior management teams, however, continue to lead in a traditional manner, and where this is the case, progress will continue to be slow.

A barrier of mistrust is also preventing progress, and this needs to be addressed at a school level and at a government level. "You are either in or out" and "them and us" were quotes from some of the teacher leaders in this study, and both resonate a state of mistrust. Furthermore, the government's relentless focus on accountability exacerbates this mistrust, and does not support teachers doing what they do best, for the good of their students and for the learning communities within which they operate. The National Education Union (2019) called for the accountability regime to be "reset and rebalanced," and I can't agree more. In order to transform school cultures, we have to disrupt the status quo and push against certain leadership approaches. Oplatka (2016) infers that a "dark side of leadership" (p. 1) is emerging in some of our schools, particularly those in challenging circumstances resulting in an "unethical school climate, a lack of social responsibility in the teacher lounge, and school failure" (p. 1). One of the teacher leaders in this study summed it up with his comment: "Whatever decisions they (SMT) make, whether you agree with it or not, you just do it!" (Karl). For cultures to change, teachers must challenge decisions they believe are not of benefit to students or the teaching profession, because if passive acceptance prevails, then change will not happen. Whilst I recognise that there can be an element of fear, we must draw on those innate qualities and beliefs that exist within teacher leaders and step bravely forward. Teachers must change their mind-set, instead of believing that they have no power, they must believe in themselves; as they are intelligent, highly trained, and highly skilled, and their voice is very important and very powerful. Teachers themselves need to be the ones to implement change, not wait for change to happen. The government could do more to help facilitate this change by helping to raise the profile of teachers and the teaching profession to gain similar status to other professions, such as in the medical profession. Furthermore, they should reduce the focus on accountability, testing, and outcomes for schools, and focus on the good work that teachers do, day to day, educating and supporting young people to become well-rounded happy individuals who make a positive contribution to society.

It is paramount that head teachers and teachers themselves identify with the concept of teacher leadership, whilst there were some in this study who understood and valued the nature of teacher leaders' work, in the main, the concept appeared under-developed. Head teachers must grasp the benefits of developing teacher leadership in their schools and recognize the positive impact that it can have on school improvement. One solution perhaps to positioning teacher leadership on their agenda could be to include it in the assessment criteria of the teaching and curriculum excellence framework for the National Professional Qualification for Head Teachers (NPQH), a qualification that most head teachers work toward. The Office for Standards in Education, Children's Services and Skills (OFSTED) also have great power to influence change in a school environment. They could support the teacher leadership agenda by referencing teacher leadership in their inspection framework. This may encourage head teachers to include developing teacher leadership as a performance indicator for the school and be motivated to gain a positive outcome in an inspection. It is critical that teachers themselves understand the nature of teacher leadership and aspire to take on those roles. Above all, teachers must force the teacher leadership agenda and look within themselves, draw on those innate qualities and desires to go above and beyond their role, and this will require a lot of effort, sometimes without additional pay.

Whilst I believe that teacher leaders possess natural, innate qualities which drive them to take on the roles that they do, whether they are effective in their role very much depends on the context within which they work. Often when the school context does not fit with the individual, they become frustrated and are quick to move, hopefully to another school, not out of the teaching profession altogether. It is widely recognised that leadership can be learned, and therefore a core part of teacher training should lend itself to developing leadership skills in a school context. I asked a trainee teacher recently who was about to start his first teaching post if he felt there were any gaps in his training, if there were any areas where he didn't feel confident or felt ill-equipped to deal with. His reply was, "I wish I knew more about how to deal with the school politics and relationships with school leaders." As a teacher educator, I reflected on the teacher training course that I teach, and realised that trainees receive no content or guidance on school leadership or developing leadership skills. Is it any wonder then that teachers aren't well versed in teacher leadership? What they learn about leadership and how they develop as a leader is often shaped by the school within which they work, and as we know from this study, good leadership is not present across all contexts, and leadership can often be extremely toxic. There is much more to be done in order to ensure that teacher leadership is firmly rooted and developed and is seen as the norm rather than the exception in all of our schools. However, this is not the work of one group of professionals, but should be driven and facilitated by government, head teachers, teacher educators, and most importantly, teachers themselves.

So, as we close this conversation, we remind ourselves and our readers that 21st-century schools need teacher leadership to forge a vision of what schools, and the teaching profession, must, by necessity, look like in order to meet the needs of a new generation of students preparing to live in an increasingly global world where national boundaries have little relevance to international needs. As a last thought, we posit that for individuals reading this book, questions and discussion need to occur in at least three areas:

1. If we take seriously Covey's (2013) idea that we need "to begin with the end in mind," we need to initiate conversations that share a vision of what is possible in the public spaces where schooling and education take place. What do we do well and where are we failing? What would teacher leadership and collaboration through professional learning communities look like in schools? How could teacher leadership as an influencing activity (Katzenmeyer & Moller, 2009) be used to improve schools and simultaneously improve the process and product of teachers' work? We must have a vision before we can begin to plan the journey.

2. If you are a teacher, you need an honest assessment of who you are, where you are both developmentally and professionally, and how can you begin to use teacher leadership to influence the issues and concerns that impact you most as a professional. Is it possible to effect real and lasting changes in the teaching profession through teacher unions and/ or teacher strikes? Why or why not?

3. And finally, if you are a principal, you need an equally honest assessment of your work as a leader. Who are you? What are your values and beliefs and how do you share those with the people who work for you? Are you willing to share your power and change the process and product of decision-making in such a way that all voices are honored through participation in meaningful, substantive ways? What is the context and school culture where you work? How do you know this to be true? What mechanisms do you use to solicit both positive and critical feedback? Is there open communication and collaboration among all major stakeholders? And thinking in concrete terms, how could you begin to support and nurture teacher leaders?

These questions are not exhaustive, but are a starting place for all teachers and principals to think about teacher leadership and its role in 21st-century schools throughout the world.

References

Blair, E. (2018). *By the light of the silvery moon: Teacher moonlighting and the dark side of teachers' work*. Gorham, ME: Myers Education Press.

Eteläpelto, A., Vähäsantanen, K., Hökkä, P. and Paloniemi, S. (2003). What is agency? Conceptualizing professional agency at work. *Educational Research Review, 10*, 45–65.

Covey, S. (2013). *The 7 habits of highly successful people: Powerful lessons in personal change* (anniversary ed.). New York: Simon & Schuster.

Garvey, M. (Author) and Martin, T. (Editor) (1986). Message to the People: The Course of African Philosophy. Dover, MA: The Majority Press, p. 98.

Katzenmeyer, M., & Moller, G. (2009). *Awakening the sleeping Giant: Helping teachers develop as leaders* (3rd ed.). Thousand Oaks, CA: Corwin Press.

Miller, E. (1999). *Educational reform in the Commonwealth Caribbean* (Interamer 54). Washington, D.C.: Organisation of American States.

National Education Union. (2019). The state of education: Workload. Retrieved from https://neu.org.uk/press-releases/state-education-workload

Oplatka, I. (2016). Irresponsible leadership" and unethical practices in schools: A conceptual framework of the "dark side" of educational leadership. In A. Normore & J. Brooks (Eds.) *The dark side of leadership: Identifying and overcoming unethical practice in organizations* (pp. 1–18). Retrieved from https://doi.org/10.1108/S1479-366020160000026001

Schlechty, P. C. (1993). On the frontier of school reform with trailblazers, pioneers, and settlers. *Journal of Staff Development, 14*(4), 46–51.

INDEX